SCOTT DELEY, CREATOR OF SCOTT'S PIZZA PROJECT

THE OONI PIZZA PROJECT

The Unofficial Guide to Making Next-Level Neapolitan, New York, Detroit and Tonda Romana Style Pizzas at Home

PAGE STREET
PUBLISHING CO.

PAGE STREET
PUBLISHING CO.

Copyright © 2023 Scott Deley

First published in 2023 by
Page Street Publishing Co.
27 Congress Street, Suite 1511
Salem, MA 01970
www.pagestreetpublishing.com

Distributed by Macmillan, sales in Canada by The Canadian Manda Group.

27 26 25 24 23   1 2 3 4 5

ISBN-13: 978-1-64567-729-1
ISBN-10: 1-64567-729-X

Library of Congress Control Number: 2022945374

Cover and book design by Molly Kate Young for Page Street Publishing Co.
Photography by Nikki Deley
Illustrations by Adobe Stock

Printed and bound in the United States

DEDICATION

I dedicate this book to my late Grandmother "Nana June," a true inspiration to me in so many ways, whose love and patience in spending so much time with me baking and cooking as a young child will be cherished forever.

TABLE OF CONTENTS

INTRODUCTION

It's fair to say that owning an Ooni pizza oven has completely changed my life! It feels like only yesterday when I came home from work and walked into my living room to unexpectedly find an Ooni Karu 12 sitting there proudly with a note from my father-in-law wishing me a happy birthday. Little did I know that in less than two years' time, I'd be an official Ooni brand ambassador, the first ever overseas guest on the *What's Good Dough?* pizza podcast and be authoring my very own pizza book. These are just a few of the memorable things that have happened to me since opening that special gift. As I write this introduction, it really makes me sit back and realize what an incredible journey it has been. By reading this book, I would love you to feel inspired to start your very own pizza journey.

Pizza is more than just food. It brings people together, sparks conversations and above all else, it makes people happy. My pizza journey began in very tough times at the start of the COVID-19 pandemic when people weren't allowed to see loved ones or mix households. This meant that I didn't get to hold my first pizza party until several months later. It was, however, well worth the wait. Seeing my friends and family all enjoying the pizzas I had made and watching them all scramble for the last slice was a moment I'll never forget. The lockdowns due to the pandemic brought widespread difficultly to everyone around the world in many different forms. I have so much to thank Ooni and pizza for, as using my Ooni pizza oven to make knockout pizzas in the comfort of my own home gave me an escape from the awful things happening around me during that time. It has become a healthy obsession, one which I have put in a lot of time and effort to try and master. Whether I'm thinking up new and exciting topping combinations or calculating how much yeast my dough requires, it's always on my mind. Very often, it will be the first thing I think of in the morning and the last thing at night.

One thing I realized while writing this book, and one of the many reasons I love pizza so much, is that every recipe has its own story. Inspiration for recipes and topping combinations can come from the most unusual and unexpected places. Throughout this book, you will be able to read where my inspirations have come from, many of which were from fond childhood memories.

In this book, you will also find a variety of my "master" dough recipes, a large selection of my favorite tried-and-tested pizza recipes (containing lots of mouth-watering flavors), as well as lots of useful information, tips and tricks on how to use and get the very best out of your Ooni pizza oven. A pizza made in an Ooni pizza oven is unique (a Neapolitan pizza takes only 60 to 90 seconds to cook) and like nothing I have tasted before, so I strive to help as many people as possible to also be able to experience this. Whether you are cooking for a crowd or just yourself, my step-by-step instructions are uncomplicated and will make it easy for you to make your own show-stopping pizzas in the comfort of your home.

The key to success is learning from the mistakes we make. So, if you make a mistake along the way, don't be disheartened. Just dust off the flour and go again. Without making mistakes I certainly wouldn't be where I am today. I'm a big believer in there being no right or wrong way when it comes to making dough and pizza . . . just a lot of different ways.

While I consider this book to be ideal if you are new to pizza making, I also believe that the more experienced pizza makers can learn a lot from it too. So whether you've made zero or thousands of pizzas, I can help you "level up" your pizza game! I'm incredibly excited to be able to share my recipes and the knowledge I have gained with you. I hope you enjoy reading this book as much as I have enjoyed writing it. It's time to throw away those takeaway pizza menus and start your very own pizza journey!

GETTING STARTED WITH YOUR OONI PIZZA OVEN

So, you've purchased your very own Ooni pizza oven! I know what you're thinking: *Now what do I do?* Don't worry, I've got you covered with everything (and I mean everything) you will need to know in your quest to making perfect pizzas at home. There are so many parts of the pizza-making process that give me a sense of immense satisfaction and joy, from seeing my beautifully smooth dough come together to when I pull a stunning homemade pizza out of the mouth of my oven. In my opinion, this feeling is unrivaled, and although I've made a huge number of pizzas since starting out, it is a feeling I look forward to every single time. One of my main goals is for you, my readers, to also experience this feeling.

In this chapter, I will give you my top tips for getting your Ooni pizza oven successfully fired up. I'll walk you through my list of essential pieces of equipment and accessories, as well as answer the most commonly asked questions I receive. After reading this chapter, I am extremely confident you'll be comfortable operating your Ooni. In no time at all, you'll be getting the same sense of satisfaction pulling your own pizzas out of your Ooni pizza oven.

Firing Up!

Whether you're using a gas, wood/charcoal or hardwood pellet-powered Ooni pizza oven, you can be ready to cook in just 15 to 20 minutes. Gas-powered ovens are extremely convenient. Once lit, just turn the flame to maximum and you'll be cooking before you know it. Always be sure to keep checking the flame is still lit during the heating-up stage.

While they can be a bit more involved due to managing the flames, wood/charcoal or pellet-powered ovens are *a lot* of fun! Beautiful, flowing flames in the back of your oven really is an incredible sight and it's extremely satisfying knowing you created them. To help get your flames roaring in your wood/charcoal or pellet oven, here are some of my top tips for you to follow:

- Make sure your chimney vent is open and chimney cap removed. If your Ooni pizza oven has a ceiling vent, open this fully too. This enables maximum airflow through your Ooni pizza oven, which in turn, will create larger, more powerful flames.

- Apart from when you check the temperature of your stone, always keep your Ooni pizza oven door on while getting up to the desired temperature.

- Make sure the fuel tray isn't overflowing when adding fuel to it.

- If you are using a wood/charcoal oven, you can use both fuel types on their own, but I recommend using them together. Start with a base layer of charcoal with 2 to 3 pieces of hardwood kindling on top and 1 or 2 natural firelighters. This will give a good, even base temperature, which you can then spike using more kindling.

- When topping up your fuel, always do this a little bit at a time and often, and wait until the flames have died down slightly. Refueling just before the flames go out is the optimal time to do this. Adding too much fuel too often will restrict the airflow inside the oven, resulting in lower temperatures.

Be Prepared!

As Benjamin Franklin once said, "Failing to prepare is preparing to fail." When embarking on your very own pizza journey, it is extremely important to make sure you have everything you need before making your first pizza. Looking back to when I started out, I found it very overwhelming when it came to knowing what to buy to go with my oven. When it comes to equipment and accessories, it's very easy to get carried away buying everything that catches your eye. Trust me, I went through this stage! So, to help you get started and to take some of the stress away, here are all the equipment and accessories I class as the "essentials," along with some helpful information thrown in to make sure you're all set up and ready to make some beautiful homemade pizzas.

Peels

With such a wide variety of pizza peels available, it is completely normal to feel daunted when deciding which is the most suited to you and your setup. Having tried many different shapes and styles, I have settled on three types, which I believe are the most suitable and cover all bases. I would suggest investing in all three, but if you would rather just buy one, I think the aluminum perforated peel is the way to go.

- **Aluminum perforated peel:** With a super-thin and smooth surface, perforated peels are the perfect "all-rounder" when it comes to peels. While being ideally suited for launching, they are also great for turning (if you are not confident enough to use a turning peel) and retrieving your pizzas. Evenly spaced perforations across the surface allow any excess flour to fall away before you launch into your oven, reducing the likelihood of a burnt base.

The ultimate Ooni setup.

An infrared thermometer will give you quick, accurate oven stone temperatures.

- **Aluminum turning peel:** Mastering how to effectively use a turning peel can be tricky, but once mastered, you'll be reaping the rewards. Not only will you look like a pro pizzaiolo, but you'll also be getting more consistent and evener bakes. It enables you to keep your pizza in contact with the stone for longer and keeps your pizza inside the oven for the duration of the bake, giving you more control in turning your pizza as well as a faster cooking time.

- **Bamboo peel:** With their smooth surface, bamboo peels are an ideal choice for launching pizzas into your oven. Not only are they great for launching, but they also double up as a great cutting and display board.

Infrared Thermometer

I can't express how important it is to know when the stone inside your Ooni pizza oven is at the optimum cooking temperature. The base of your pizza is a key element in achieving pizza perfection, and this is all down to getting the stone inside your oven to the correct temperature for the style of pizza you are making. You can also use an infrared thermometer to check the temperature of your dough if you don't have a probe thermometer.

Accurate Weighing Scales

When making any of my four master dough recipes in this book, you will notice that certain ingredients require weighing to one or two decimal places. It might seem crazy having to weigh out ingredients to this degree, but the accuracy of your measurements will have a big effect on the quality of your dough. For example, using 0.5 gram more yeast than specified could mean your dough over ferments and becomes unusable.

A stiff bristled brush will make clean-up a breeze.

Plastic Dough Scraper

Whether you choose to make your dough by hand or use a stand/spiral mixer, there will always be a need to scrape around the inside of your bowl to remove any dried bits of flour and dough. These dough scrapers are also extremely handy in removing your dough from the bowl after mixing, as well as after bulk fermentation.

Room Thermometer

Achieving the perfect dough is dependent on many things, but one of the most important is knowing the temperature of the room your dough will be fermented in. This enables you to accurately calculate the amount of yeast required. I recommend using a digital thermometer that you can move from room to room depending on where you choose to leave your dough to ferment. Here's a good tip to get an accurate average room temperature: For the 24 hours before you make your dough, keep your eye on the thermometer every few hours to see how the temperature varies.

Heatproof Gloves

When working with temperatures of up to 930°F (500°C), it's important to keep your hands protected. Whether you're topping up your fuel, removing the pizza oven door, cleaning your Ooni pizza oven stone or using cast-iron skillets, you will be subjecting your hands to extreme heat. Protection is essential; investing in a good pair of heatproof gloves helps you safely sling pizzas like a pro!

Cleaning Brush

After each pizza, there will be excess flour and maybe some fallen toppings on your stone. There will also be the odd disaster (it happens to us all), so having a stiff bristled cleaning brush on hand to give the stone a quick clean after cooking will keep the stone clean and ready for your next batch of pizzas.

Bowl/Containers

A stand/spiral mixer will come with its own mixing bowl, but if you are making your dough by hand, I recommend using a medium-sized mixing bowl. The bowl I use when making the amount of dough specified in this book is 9 inches (23 cm) in diameter and 5 inches (13 cm) deep. This will give your dough enough space to ferment and rise.

Once you have balled up your dough after bulk fermentation, you will need to put the balls into individual airtight containers or an airtight dough tray. If using individual containers, I recommend using ones that are approximately 6 inches (15 cm) in diameter and 2 inches (5 cm) deep. If you prefer to use a dough tray, one that is approximately 16 inches (40 cm) long and 12 inches (30 cm) wide is an ideal size for holding 4 to 6 dough balls.

Fuel

Whichever Ooni pizza oven you are using, it's important to use the right type of wood, charcoal or pellets to ensure you can reach those high temperatures with a nice clean flame. If you are using wood and charcoal to fuel your oven, you should use kiln-dried hardwood (beech or oak are ideal) and lumpwood charcoal. If you are using pellets, low-moisture, 100-percent hardwood pellets are the way to go. Softwood pellets burn a lot quicker than hardwood pellets and produce more smoke and soot.

It's important to store your fuel(s) in an airtight container to prevent any moisture from being absorbed, which would affect the burn.

Pizza Oven Cover

All Ooni pizza ovens are designed to be stored outdoors. To protect it from the elements, it's a good idea to keep it under an Ooni pizza oven cover. These covers are specifically designed to fit your oven, are waterproof and are made using breathable materials, making them ideal to protect your oven when not in use. Always make sure your oven is dry and has completely cooled down before covering.

Cast-iron skillets are a great accessory for cooking meat and vegetables in the Ooni.

Cast-Iron Skillet

You can make so much more than just pizza in your Ooni pizza ovens. Cast-iron skillets are the perfect accessory to cook all kinds of meat, vegetables and so much more. I've even baked chocolate chip skillet cookies and a banana loaf using mine. The possibilities are endless.

Commonly Asked Questions

Whether you're completely new to pizza-making or not, there will always be questions that pop into your head. Through my social media channels, I spend a lot of time answering all sorts of questions, so I wanted to include some of the most common to help you along the way and to make sure your pizza-making experience is as fun as possible. So, whether you're wondering why your pizza is burning or why it's sticking to your peel, I've got you covered.

How do you keep your stone so clean?

I recommend cleaning your stone after each pizza. There will always be some excess burnt flour on the stone after you have taken your pizza out of your oven. Using your oven brush and heatproof gloves, loosen the flour off the stone and brush it to the back of the oven so it is close to the flames. Being so close to the flames will help it burn off while you are preparing your next pizza. If you have stubborn stains, continue to run your pizza oven at maximum for 10 to 15 minutes after the last pizza has cooked. This will burn off the flour and stains, leaving you with a nice clean stone ready for next time. Alternatively, you can flip your stone each time you use your oven so that the stained side is facing down. The high temperatures inside the oven will clean the underside of the stone while you are cooking.

Why is the underside of my pizza burning?

This could be one or a combination of the following three things:

- **Too much flour on your peel when launching:** When flour lands on a hot stone, it will burn, so it's important to only use a small amount of flour on your peel. I recommend using fine semolina flour as the grains act like mini ball bearings, meaning you need less to achieve a nice, smooth launch. Using a perforated peel also makes a big difference. The perforations allow excess flour to fall away before you launch your pizza into your oven.

- **Stone temperature is too high:** As all Ooni pizza ovens can reach temperatures greater than 930°F (500°C), it's important to closely monitor this with an infrared thermometer. If you are finding the underside of your pizza is burning, try lowering the stone temperature slightly, before you launch your pizza.

- **Keep turning:** After you have launched your pizza into the oven, don't wait too long to get it moving and make your first turn. Rotating more frequently will mean the pizza has not sat for as long on the hot stone. In all the recipes in this book, I give you the recommended times to make all of your turns and the signs to look out for before making a turn . . . so be sure to look out for those.

How do I stop my pizzas burning at the back of the oven?

The timing of your first turn is essential in getting an even bake on your crust. A matter of seconds can be the difference between a perfectly baked pizza and one that is completely burnt. After you have launched your pizza, don't take your eyes off it for one second. The pizza needs your complete attention while it's being cooked, so don't be tempted to start work on the next one while you have one in the oven. As soon as you see the crust at the back of the oven start to brown/blister, get that pizza moving.

How do I stop my pizza sticking to the peel on launch?

- It's important that your dough is at room temperature when you stretch it out and place it onto your peel. Cold dough is more likely to stick, which will make launching into your oven more difficult.

- Adding a small amount of flour/semolina flour to your peel will help stop the dough from sticking. I recommend sprinkling it from a height to ensure you get a nice, even coverage on your peel. Right before you launch your pizza into your oven, give your peel a quick shake to make sure the pizza is moving freely. If it is sticking, lift the edge of the pizza, and add a little more flour.

- You should never rush pizza making, as this prevents you from enjoying the experience, but try not to leave the pizza on your peel for too long before you launch it. The longer it remains on the peel, the more of a chance it absorbs the flour and sticks. I recommend topping your pizza before transferring it to your peel. This will reduce the amount of time the dough is on the peel before you launch it into your oven.

What is the secret to achieving a nice, round base?

Once balled up, it's important to always keep your dough nice and round. If at any point you lose the circular shape, stop and give it a quick reshape. I cover the stretching process in each recipe, giving you all my tips and tricks on how to achieve a perfectly round pizza. One of the key steps is to reshape the pizza directly before you launch into your oven as transferring the pizza to your peel will usually influence its shape.

What should I do if I tear a hole in my dough?

This happens to everyone, so don't worry. Place your dough down onto the countertop and pinch the sides of the hole together with your fingertips, and flatten it back down using a little sprinkle of flour/semolina flour. If your pizza needs further stretching out after this, take extra care to avoid further tears.

How do I stop tearing my Neapolitan pizza on the first turn?

As Neapolitan pizzas are fully cooked in 60 to 90 seconds, timing the first turn can be tricky. It's important to give your pizza enough time after launch before making your first turn. If you attempt the first turn too soon, the chances of tearing it increase. I find 20 seconds to be the optimum amount of time. This should be enough time for the base to begin to set, meaning you can carefully slide your peel cleanly underneath. If you are using a turning peel, carefully slide it under each half of the pizza to release it from the stone before making your first turn. Whichever peel you choose, warming it up in the flames at the back of the oven will help when sliding it underneath the pizza for the first time.

How do I stop the center of my pizza rising from the pizza oven stone while cooking?

This is generally caused by the base of your pizza being too thin in the center compared to the outer areas. When stretching your dough over your knuckles, make sure you keep your hands to the edge and keep the dough rotating so that it isn't hanging in the same position for too long. This will give more of an even stretch. However, if the center of your pizza does start to rise during the bake, carefully slide your peel under your pizza to release the trapped air.

Why does my dough keep shrinking back when I'm stretching it out prior to topping?

This is usually a sign that your dough balls aren't relaxed enough and require more time at room temperature. For example, if you have balled up your dough into individual dough balls and allowed them to rest for four hours, next time reduce your bulk fermentation time by an hour or two and let the dough balls rest for five or six hours, especially if it's a cooler day.

MASTER DOUGHS
AND SIMPLE SAUCE

The foundation of any great pizza comes from the dough and the sauce. Pizza dough is more than just the base of your pizza; it's what brings everything together while also holding an incredible amount of flavor and texture. If done well, you will be well on your way to achieving incredible results, whatever style of pizza you decide to make. In this chapter, you will find my master dough recipes for my four favorite types of pizza: Neapolitan, New York, Detroit Style (DSP) and Tonda Romana. You will also find my Keep-It-Simple Tomato Sauce recipe (page 35) which only uses three ingredients. I wanted to make sure there was a wide variety of pizza dough styles in this book, so whether a soft, light and airy dough is your preference or a thin and crispy one, you'll find it all here with everything in between thrown in for good measure.

When looking through my dough recipes, you may be surprised by the small amount of yeast required as well as the accuracy required in measuring it. The amount of yeast required in any type of dough is dependent on the length of time it is left to ferment and the temperature of the environment (kitchen, refrigerator, etc.) it is fermenting in. Getting the fermentation process correct is the most important element in achieving a beautiful, flavorsome dough, so I can't stress enough how important it is to be accurate when weighing out all your ingredients, including the liquid ingredients (water and oil). Each of my dough recipes require 24 hours of fermentation at room temperature. I have calculated the amount of yeast required using an average room temperature of 64.4°F (18°C). If your room is warmer or cooler than this, I recommend using the "Ooni Calculator" app to calculate the exact amount of yeast you require. This calculator can also be used to increase or decrease the amount of dough required to match the number of pizzas you wish to make.

NEAPOLITAN DOUGH

YIELD: 4 (11" [28-cm]) pizzas

677 g 00 flour
0.34 g instant dried yeast
426 g water
17 g salt
Fine semolina flour

It is usually the toppings used on a pizza which steal the limelight, but the key to any great pizza is the dough. If you can master this and add great toppings into the equation, then the result will be like nothing you've experienced before. A perfectly executed Neapolitan pizza is easily my favorite food, and from the first day of owning my Ooni pizza oven it was something I was determined to master. True Neapolitan pizza dough is made using only four simple ingredients (flour, water, salt and yeast). There are, however, MANY different processes you can follow when trying to make it. I have lost count of the amount of different dough experiments I have carried out in my quest to achieve Neapolitan pizza perfection, but this recipe I am sharing with you is as good as it gets in my opinion. By meticulously following my step-by-step process and using all my tips and tricks, you too will be making authentic Neapolitan pizzas with those iconic light, airy and digestible crusts together with beautiful slightly charred bubbles on the surface of the crusts (aka leoparding).

Weigh the flour, yeast, water and salt. The water can be used straight from the tap and doesn't need to be warm, especially if you're using a stand/spiral mixer. The friction of the machine generates heat, which can affect the final temperature of the dough. Also, since we are fermenting for 24 hours, we want to control the yeast so it is not too active. If you are making dough in very warm conditions (for example, in a room above 75°F [24°C]), I recommend putting your water in the fridge for a few hours so that the final temperature of the kneaded dough isn't too high. Ideally you are looking for a dough temperature of 68 to 73°F (20 to 23°C).

In your bowl, add the flour and yeast and mix just to combine. While mixing on low speed, or by hand, gradually add 95 percent (405 g) of the water until the dough has come together and formed a rough-looking ball. This should take 2 to 3 minutes. If there are any bits of flour around the edge that haven't been incorporated, scrape around the inside of the bowl with a plastic dough scraper. Cover the bowl with a towel (dry or damp), and let the dough rest for 20 minutes. Resting the dough at this point will hydrate the flour and encourage the gluten development to begin.

Add the salt and a splash of the remaining water. Turn the mixer on to medium speed. Gradually add the remaining water and mix for approximately 7 to 8 minutes until the water has been absorbed and the dough starts to have a smoother consistency. It is important to gradually add the water, as too much at once will result in your dough being spun around by the dough hook rather than kneaded. If mixing by hand, once you have added the salt and water and mixed until the water has been absorbed, turn the dough out onto a clean countertop and knead for 8 to 10 minutes until smooth and not tacky to the touch.

(continued)

NEAPOLITAN DOUGH (CONTINUED)

If you have a thermometer, it's a good idea to check the temperature of the dough at this stage. The dough should be 68 to 73°F (20 to 23°C). If your dough is less than 68°F (20°C), continue to knead/mix until you reach this temperature. Don't worry if your dough has gone past this temperature range; it just means you will need to be a little more careful when stretching out the dough ball before topping so it doesn't tear.

Take the dough out of the mixing bowl (if using a stand/spiral mixer) and form it into a ball on a clean countertop. Don't be tempted to add flour to the countertop, as this will affect the hydration of the dough. Cover the dough with a towel (dry or damp), and let it rest directly on the countertop for 15 to 30 minutes. This rest period allows the dough to relax and helps you achieve a nice, smooth ball in the next step.

Uncover the dough, and with both hands, lift it off the countertop and fold it over three to four times, rotating 90 degrees after each fold (refer to photo 1).

After the final fold, pull the dough toward you to shape it into a smooth ball (refer to photo 2).

If mixing by hand or in a standard stand mixer, repeat this step another two to three times, covering and resting for 15 minutes after each time. This technique of stretching and folding the dough will increase the tension and build up the strength of the dough, which in turn, will help prevent your individual dough balls from collapsing and going flat during the second stage of fermentation. This step is not necessary if you are using a professional spiral mixer.

After the final set of stretch and folds, transfer the dough to a lightly oiled, airtight container, and let the dough ferment at room temperature for 18 to 20 hours. Adding the oil will help when you remove the dough from the container.

After 18 to 20 hours, the dough should have risen considerably. Remove from the container, and using a dough cutter, divide the dough into four equal-sized portions (approximately 275 grams each). With your hands, form the dough portions into tight balls. To do this, hold the portion of dough in your hands with your fingers curled around the edges and fold the dough in half inward (refer to photo 3).

Repeat this step several times, rotating 90 degrees each time. Once the dough ball is nice and smooth with a tight outer surface, pinch the bottom of the dough ball to seal (refer to photo 4). This will help your dough balls achieve a nice rise during this second stage of fermentation. If the dough is a little sticky and difficult to work with when forming the balls, put a little bit of cold water on your hands.

Transfer the dough balls into lightly oiled, individual, airtight containers or an airtight dough tray for 4 to 6 hours at room temperature. Adding the oil will help maintain the balls' round shape when you remove them. If you are not ready to make your pizzas 4 to 6 hours after balling up your dough, you can transfer the dough balls to the fridge where they will keep for a further 24 hours. In my experience, doing this will result in more prominent blisters (leoparding) on the crust. So, if like me, that is what you strive for, I would recommend doing this. The dough will be much more relaxed, meaning a gentler touch and more care will be required when stretching out the dough. You will need to remove the dough balls from the fridge at least 3 hours before using, to allow them to come back up to room temperature.

After 4 to 6 hours at room temperature (or 3 hours after removing from the fridge), tip out your dough ball from the container (or remove it from the dough tray) onto a bed of fine semolina flour. (If you don't have fine semolina, you can use normal 00 flour that you used to make your dough.) Cover the dough with some extra semolina so it is coated and not sticky to touch. If the dough has lost its circular shape, reshape it at this point. From the center, using your fingers, carefully push the dough down and out toward the edge leaving a ½-inch (1-cm) crust. Keep rotating the dough as you do this to maintain its circular shape as this will impact the final shape of your pizza once it is cooked (refer to photo 5).

Flip the dough over and continue to stretch it out using this technique. At this point, make sure you don't flip the dough over again as this is the side we want as the top of the pizza. (This was the side that was at the top when in the individual container or dough tray.) Once the dough has been stretched as far as possible using this technique, pick the dough up, and carefully toss it from one hand to the other a few times to remove some of the excess flour. Hang the dough up right over both sets of your knuckles and begin to rotate the dough through your hands, allowing gravity to stretch it out (refer to photo 6).

Make sure it is the outer edge (just inside the formed crust) that hangs off your knuckles. It's important not to stretch from the center as this will cause the base to be too thin, causing it to tear. Once the dough is evenly stretched to about 11 inches (28 cm) with a nice, thin base, scrape most of the semolina flour to one side of your surface and place the dough back down onto the countertop. The dough is now ready to be topped.

NEW YORK DOUGH

YIELD: 4 (11" [28-cm]) pizzas

464 g strong bread flour
124 g 00 flour
31 g fine semolina flour
0.42 g instant dried yeast
390 g water
15 g salt
15 g extra virgin olive oil

New York pizzas are immensely popular throughout the world and something I've strived to master ever since starting out on my pizza journey. I've experimented a lot with this style of dough, most of the time because I always felt there was something missing. Sometimes it would be a lack of flavor, other times it would relate to the texture or color of the dough. It wasn't until I started to combine different percentages of different types of flour that I really started to feel that I was onto a winner. My winning flour combination and the recipe I'm sharing with you is made up of 75 percent strong bread flour (gives the dough a chewy robust texture), 20 percent 00 flour (gives the dough elasticity) and 5 percent fine semolina flour (gives the dough some extra crunch). With New York dough being more robust than other doughs, don't forget to give it a toss into the air at the end of the stretching process!

Weigh the flours, yeast, water, salt and oil. The water can be used straight from the tap and doesn't need to be warm, especially if you're using a stand/spiral mixer. The friction of the machine generates heat, which can affect the final temperature of the dough. Also, since we are fermenting for 24 hours, we want to control the yeast so it is not too active. If you are making dough in very warm conditions (for example, in a room above 75°F [24°C]), I recommend putting your water in the fridge for a few hours so that the final temperature of the kneaded dough isn't too high. Ideally, you are looking for a dough temperature of 68 to 73°F (20 to 23°C).

In your bowl, add the three types of flour and yeast and mix just to combine. While mixing on low speed, or by hand, gradually add 95 percent (356 g) of the water until the dough has come together and formed a rough-looking ball. This should take 2 to 3 minutes. If there are any bits of flour around the edge that haven't been incorporated, scrape around the inside of the bowl with a plastic dough scraper. Cover the bowl with a towel (dry or damp), and let the dough rest for 20 minutes. Resting the dough at this point will hydrate the flour and encourage the gluten development to begin.

Add the salt and a splash of the remaining water. Turn the mixer on to medium speed. Gradually add the remaining water and mix for approximately 7 to 8 minutes until the water has been absorbed and the dough starts to have a smoother consistency. It is important to gradually add the water, as too much at once will result in your dough being spun around by the dough hook rather than kneaded. If mixing by hand, once you have added the salt and water and mixed until the water has been absorbed, turn the dough out onto a clean countertop and knead for 7 to 8 minutes until smooth and not tacky to touch.

(continued)

NEW YORK DOUGH (CONTINUED)

Add the oil and mix in the mixer on low or knead by hand on a clean countertop for 3 minutes until the oil has been fully absorbed. If you have a thermometer, it's a good idea to check the temperature of the dough at this stage. The dough should be 68 to 73°F (20 to 23°C). If your dough is less than 68°F (20°C), continue to knead/mix until you reach this temperature. Don't worry if your dough has gone past this temperature range; it just means you will need to be a little more careful when stretching out the dough ball before topping so it doesn't tear.

Take the dough out of the mixing bowl (if using a stand/spiral mixer) and form it into a ball on a clean countertop. Don't be tempted to add flour to the countertop, as this will affect the hydration of the dough. Cover the dough with a towel (dry or damp), and let it rest directly on the countertop for 15 to 30 minutes. This rest period allows the dough to relax and helps you achieve a nice, smooth ball in the next step.

Uncover the dough, and with both hands, lift it off the countertop and fold it over three to four times, rotating 90 degrees after each fold (refer to photo 1 in Neapolitan dough recipe on page 20).

After the final fold, pull the dough toward you to shape it into a smooth ball (refer to photo 2 in Neapolitan dough recipe on page 20).

If mixing by hand or in a standard stand mixer, repeat this step another two to three times, covering and resting for 15 minutes after each time. This technique of stretching and folding the dough will increase the tension and build up the strength of the dough, which in turn, will help prevent your individual dough balls from collapsing and going flat during the second stage of fermentation. This step is not necessary if you are using a professional spiral mixer.

After the final set of stretch and folds, transfer the dough to a lightly oiled, airtight container, and let the dough ferment at room temperature for 1 hour. Adding the oil will help when you remove the dough from the container.

After 1 hour, the dough should have risen slightly. Remove from the container, and using a dough cutter, divide the dough into four equal-sized portions (approximately 260 grams each).

With your hands, form the dough portions into tight balls. To do this, hold the portion of dough in your hands with your fingers curled around the edges and fold the dough in half inward (refer to photo 3 in Neapolitan dough recipe on page 20).

Repeat this step several times, rotating 90 degrees each time. Once the dough ball is nice and smooth with a tight outer surface, pinch the bottom of the dough ball to seal (refer to photo 4 in Neapolitan dough recipe on page 20). This will help your dough balls achieve a nice rise during this second stage of fermentation. If the dough is a little sticky and difficult to work with when forming the balls, put a little bit of cold water on your hands.

Transfer the dough balls into lightly oiled, individual, airtight containers or an airtight dough tray for 1 hour at room temperature. Adding the oil will help maintain the balls' round shape when you remove them. After 1 hour, transfer the dough balls to the fridge for 24 to 48 hours. You will need to remove the dough balls from the fridge at least 3 hours before using to allow them to come back up to room temperature.

Tip out your room-temperature dough ball from the container (or remove it from the dough tray) onto a bed of fine semolina flour. (If you don't have fine semolina, you can use normal 00 flour that you used to make your dough.) Cover the dough with some extra semolina so it is coated and not sticky to touch. If the dough has lost its circular shape, reshape it at this point.

As New York pizzas have a smaller crust compared to Neapolitan, instead of pushing all the air from the center to the edge, it is important to form the crust first. Do this by using your fingertips to press all the way around the edge leaving a ½-inch (1-cm) gap inward (refer to photo 1).

Flatten out the center of the dough with your hands, which will begin to stretch it out. Keep rotating the dough as you do this to maintain its circular shape as this will impact the final shape of your pizza once it is cooked. Flip the dough over and continue to stretch it out using this technique. At this point, make sure you don't flip the dough over again as this is the side we want as the top of the pizza. (This was the side that was at the top when in the individual container.) Once the dough has been stretched as far as possible using this technique, pick the dough up and carefully toss it from one hand to the other a few times to remove some of the excess flour. Hang the dough upright over both sets of your knuckles and begin to rotate the dough through your hands, allowing gravity to stretch it out (refer to photo 6 in Neapolitan dough recipe on page 21).

Make sure it is the outer edge (just inside the formed crust) that hangs off your knuckles. It's important not to stretch from the center as this will cause the base to be too thin, causing it to tear.

If you're feeling confident, toss the dough into the air while making sure to keep your fingers rolled in to avoid piercing the dough. Once the dough is evenly stretched to about 11 inches (28 cm) with a nice, thin base, scrape most of the semolina flour to one side of your surface and place the dough back down onto the countertop. The dough is now ready to be topped.

DETROIT DOUGH

YIELD: 1 (8 x 10" (20 x 25-cm) pizza

220 g high-protein flour (at least 11.5 percent)

0.12 g instant dried yeast

145 g water

5.5 g salt

5 g butter

30 g extra virgin olive oil, plus extra for dimpling the dough

Detroit pizza dough is typically made using a higher percentage of water (referred to as the dough's "hydration"), normally around the 70 to 80-percent mark. You can, however, still achieve great results using a lower hydration. After a lot of experimentation, I have found that 66-percent hydration is the perfect number for me. This still gives a light, airy dough, while being much easier to handle compared to a dough at a higher hydration, particularly if you are mixing by hand. For the Detroit pizza pan, I highly recommend investing in an anodized aluminum pan specifically designed for this style of pizza. These can withstand higher temperatures and are layered with a coating to make releasing the pizza a lot easier. You can use a normal baking pan, but this will make it difficult to achieve the iconic cheese wall or "frico," as it is more commonly known, which you will see in all my Detroit pizza recipes.

Weigh out the flour, yeast, water and salt. The water can be used straight from the tap and doesn't need to be warm, especially if you're using a stand/spiral mixer. The friction of the machine generates heat, which can affect the final temperature of the dough. Also, since we are fermenting for 24 hours, we want to control the yeast so it is not too active. If you are making dough in very warm conditions (for example, in a room above 75°F [24°C]), I recommend putting your water in the fridge for a few hours so that the final temperature of the kneaded dough isn't too high. Ideally, you are looking for a dough temperature of 68 to 73°F (20 to 23°C).

In your bowl, add the flour and yeast and mix just to combine. While mixing on a low speed, or by hand, gradually add 95 percent (209 g) of the water until the dough has come together and formed a rough-looking ball. This should take 2 to 3 minutes. If there are any bits of flour around the edge that haven't been incorporated, scrape around the inside of the bowl with a plastic dough scraper. Cover the bowl with a towel (dry or damp), and let the dough rest for 20 minutes. Resting the dough at this point will hydrate the flour and encourage the gluten development to begin.

Add the salt and a splash of the remaining water and turn the mixer back on to a medium speed. Gradually add the remaining water and mix for approximately 7 to 8 minutes until the water has been absorbed and the dough starts to have a smoother consistency. It is important to gradually add the water, as too much at once will result in your dough being spun around by the dough hook rather than kneaded. If mixing by hand, once you have added the salt and water and mixed until the water has been absorbed, turn the dough out onto a clean countertop and knead for 8 to 10 minutes until smooth and not tacky to the touch.

(continued)

DETROIT DOUGH (CONTINUED)

If you have a thermometer, it's a good idea to check the temperature of the dough at this stage. The dough should be 68 to 73°F (20 to 23°C). If your dough is less than 68°F (20°C), continue to knead/mix until you reach this temperature. Don't worry if your dough has gone past this temperature range; it just means you will need to be a little more careful when stretching out the dough ball before topping so it doesn't tear.

Take the dough out of the mixing bowl (if using a stand/spiral mixer) and form it into a ball on a clean countertop. Don't be tempted to add flour to the countertop, as this will affect the hydration of the dough. Cover the dough with a towel (dry or damp), and let it rest directly on the countertop for 15 to 30 minutes. This rest period allows the dough to relax and helps you achieve a nice, smooth ball in the next step. Uncover the dough and with both hands, lift it off the countertop and fold it over three to four times, rotating 90 degrees after each fold (refer to photo 1 in Neapolitan dough recipe on page 20).

After the final fold, pull the dough toward you to shape it into a smooth ball (refer to photo 2 in Neapolitan dough recipe on page 20).

If mixing by hand or in a standard stand mixer, repeat this step another two to three times, covering and resting for 15 minutes after each time. This technique of stretching and folding the dough will increase the tension and build up the strength of the dough. This step is not necessary if you are using a professional spiral mixer.

After the final set of stretch and folds, transfer the dough to a lightly oiled, airtight container, and let the dough ferment at room temperature for 16 to 18 hours. Adding the oil will help when you remove the dough from the container.

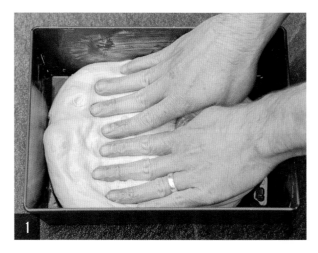

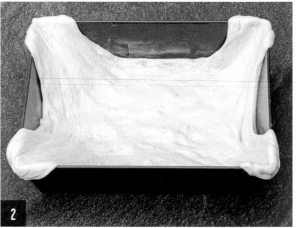

After 16 to 18 hours, the dough should have risen considerably. Evenly smear the butter on the bottom and the sides of the pan, and then add the oil, spreading it around with your hands. Transfer the dough into the pan, making sure the smooth side is at the bottom. Flip the dough over so it is evenly coated in oil, and then, with your fingertips, gently press the dough down so it starts to spread toward the corners (refer to photo 1).

It is unlikely the dough will reach the corners straight away, but this is not a problem. Simply cover the pan and let the dough rest in a warm spot for 20 to 30 minutes, and then press the dough down again until it reaches the corners. If required, you can repeat this step two to three times. To get distinct, sharp corners once the pizza is cooked, I recommend lifting the four corners of the dough and carefully hooking them over the corners of the pan (refer to photo 2).

Leave them in this position for 30 to 45 seconds, and then carefully unhook them and allow them to fall back into position (refer to photo 3).

Cover the dough and let it rest for 6 to 8 hours. (You should see a slight rise in the dough.) Uncover the dough 30 minutes before cooking, and drizzle some oil over it and on your hands. "Dimple" the dough by spreading your fingers slightly and gently pressing them down into the dough (refer to photo 4).

This will create air bubbles, making your dough nice and light when baked. Cover the dough, and let it rest in a warm spot for 30 minutes. After 30 minutes, the dough is ready to par-bake.

TONDA ROMANA DOUGH

YIELD: 4 (11" [28-cm]) pizzas

433 g 00 flour
0.23 g instant dried yeast
251 g water
8.7 g salt
6 g extra virgin olive oil

Tonda Romana is a very thin style of pizza with a crunchy, cracker-like crust. The crunchy texture is achieved by using a lower hydration (I use 58-percent) compared to Neapolitan dough. It is stretched out using a rolling pin and baked at a lower temperature (715°F [380°C]) for slightly longer. Every time I make this style of pizza, I look forward to the sound made when I first roll my pizza cutter through the crispy crust! These pizzas are perfect if you are not a lover of the bigger, fluffier crusts or if you are just looking for something a little lighter on the stomach. Due to the lower hydration (making it less sticky), this dough is very easy to handle, so it is a good dough if you are new to pizza making. I always recommend that newcomers start with a lower hydration to build up their confidence in handling and working the dough before moving on to the more advanced dough recipes.

Weigh out the flour, yeast, water, salt and oil. The water can be used straight from the tap and doesn't need to be warm, especially if you're using a stand/spiral mixer. The friction of the machine generates heat, which can affect the final temperature of the dough. Also, since we are fermenting for 24 hours, we want to control the yeast so it is not too active. If you are making dough in very warm conditions (for example, in a room above 75°F [24°C]), I recommend putting your water in the fridge for a few hours so that the final temperature of the kneaded dough isn't too high. Ideally you are looking for a dough temperature of 68 to 73°F (20 to 23°C).

In your bowl, add the flour and yeast and mix just to combine. While mixing on a low speed, or by hand, gradually add 95 percent (238 g) of the water until the dough has come together and formed a rough-looking ball. This should take 2 to 3 minutes. If there are any bits of flour around the edge that haven't been incorporated, scrape around the inside of the bowl with a plastic dough scraper.

Add the salt and a splash of the remaining water. Turn the mixer on to medium speed. Gradually add the remaining water and mix for approximately 5 to 7 minutes until the water has been absorbed and the dough starts to have a smoother consistency. It is important to gradually add the water, as too much at once will result in your dough being spun around by the dough hook rather than kneaded. If mixing by hand, once you have added the salt and water and mixed until the water has been absorbed, turn the dough out onto a clean countertop and knead for 5 minutes until smooth and not tacky to the touch.

(continued)

TONDA ROMANA DOUGH (CONTINUED)

Add the oil and mix in the mixer on low or knead by hand on a clean countertop for 2 to 3 minutes, or until the oil has been fully absorbed and the dough is not tacky to the touch. If you have a thermometer, it's a good idea to check the temperature of the dough at this stage. The dough should be 68 to 73°F (20 to 23°C). If your dough is less than 68°F (20°C), continue to knead/mix until you reach this temperature. Don't worry if your dough has gone past this temperature range; it just means you will need to be a little more careful when stretching out the dough ball before topping so it doesn't tear.

Take the dough out of the mixing bowl (if using a stand/spiral mixer) and form it into a ball on a clean countertop. Don't be tempted to add flour to the countertop, as this will affect the hydration of the dough. Cover the dough with a towel (dry or damp), and let it rest directly on the countertop for 15 to 30 minutes. This rest period allows the dough to relax and helps you achieve a nice, smooth ball in the next step.

Uncover the dough, and with both hands, pull the dough toward you two to three times, lifting and turning the dough 180 degrees each time, to shape it into a tight, smooth ball (refer to photo 2 in Neapolitan dough recipe on page 20).

Transfer the dough to a lightly oiled, airtight container, and let the dough ferment at room temperature for 18 hours. Adding the oil will help when you remove the dough from the container.

After 18 hours, the dough should have risen considerably. Remove from the container and using a dough cutter, divide the dough into four equal-sized portions (approximately 170 grams each). With your hands, form the dough portions into tight balls. To do this, hold the portion of dough in your hands with your fingers curled around the edges and fold the dough in half inward (refer to photo 3 in Neapolitan dough recipe on page 20).

Repeat this step several times, rotating 90 degrees each time. Once the dough ball is nice and smooth with a tight outer surface, pinch the bottom of the dough ball to seal (refer to photo 4 in Neapolitan dough recipe on page 20). This will help your dough balls achieve a nice rise during this second stage of fermentation.

Transfer the dough balls into lightly oiled, individual, airtight containers or an airtight dough tray for 6 hours at room temperature. Adding the oil will help maintain the balls' round shape when you remove them. If you are not ready to make your pizzas 4 to 6 hours after balling up your dough, you can transfer the dough balls to the fridge where they will keep for a further 48 hours. You will need to remove the dough balls from the fridge at least 3 hours before using to allow them to come back up to room temperature.

After 6 hours at room temperature (or 3 hours after removing from the fridge), tip out your dough ball from the containers (or remove them from the dough tray) onto a bed of fine semolina flour. (If you don't have fine semolina, you can use normal 00 flour that you used to make your dough.) Cover the dough with some extra semolina so it is coated and not sticky to touch. If the dough has lost its circular shape, reshape it at this point.

As this style of pizza does not have a prominent crust like a Neapolitan, it requires a different technique to stretch it out. From the center, with your fingers, carefully push the dough down and out going all the way to the edge (refer to photo 1). Do not leave any crust.

Keep rotating the dough as you do this to maintain its circular shape as this will impact the final shape of your pizza once it is cooked. Now flip the dough over and continue to stretch it out using this technique. Make sure you don't flip the dough over again as this is the side we want as the top of the pizza. (This was the side that was at the top when in the individual container.) With your rolling pin, roll out the dough as thinly as possible, rotating as you go to maintain the circular shape (refer to photo 2).

Once the dough has been stretched as far as possible, pick the dough up and carefully toss it from one hand to the other a few times to remove some of the excess flour. Hang the dough over the backs of your open hands and start to move your hands apart while rotating to stretch out the dough (refer to photo 3).

Once the dough is evenly stretched to about 11 inches (28 cm) with a nice, thin base, scrape most of the semolina flour to one side of your surface and place the dough back down onto the countertop. To finish off the dough, use your fingers to gently press all the way around the edge of the dough to ensure it's as thin as possible. Don't be tempted to pop any little air bubbles in the crust as they will char up in the oven, giving you even more of that lovely crunch! The dough is now ready to be topped.

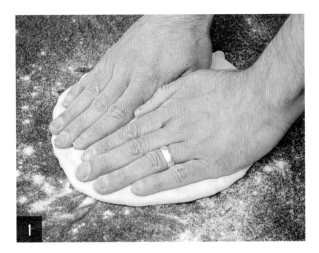

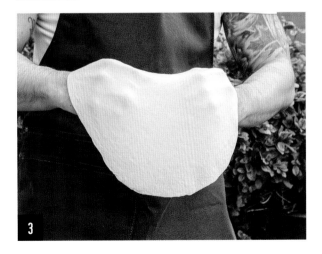

KEEP-IT-SIMPLE TOMATO SAUCE

YIELD: enough sauce for 3–4 (11" [28 cm]) pizzas

1 (14-oz [400-g]) can San Marzano Tomatoes

1 tsp salt

Fresh basil leaves, finely chopped

Making the perfect tomato sauce for all types of pizzas is all about simplicity. If you use good-quality tomatoes, keeping it simple allows their beautiful flavor to do the talking! When I first started out, I experimented with many different recipes for tomato sauce. I reduced the sauce down, added sugar, oil, garlic and multiple herb combinations, but I always came back to the simple combination of salt, a little basil, and importantly, no cooking. When added to a pizza and cooked in the Ooni pizza oven, the tomatoes will be exposed to temperatures up to 930°F (500°C), so cooking them beforehand could result in a bitter flavor. Some argue that adding basil to the sauce is a step too far, but I love the flavor it gives, and I believe it elevates this sauce from the rest! Don't throw the empty can of tomatoes away; they make great-looking pots to grow your very own basil plants!

Remove the tomatoes from the can, reserving the liquid. In a sieve, gently squeeze the tomatoes to release any liquid. This keeps the sauce from becoming too watery. To make sure the sauce has a nice consistency, remove any tough stem ends from the tomatoes, and discard.

Place your tomatoes into a bowl and add the juice from the can. Add the salt, and with an immersion blender, blend using very short pulses. You will only need two or three pulses to get to the perfect consistency; any more than this may introduce too much oxygen into the sauce and give it a bitter taste while also affecting the color. If you don't have an immersion blender, you can use a food mill or simply break the tomatoes down with your hands. Add the basil and stir to combine. You can use the sauce right away or put it into an airtight container and store in the fridge for up to 3 days. Allow the sauce to come to room temperature before using.

NEAPOLITAN

If I close my eyes and think of pizza, it will be a Neapolitan pizza 99.9-percent of the time, which just goes to show that without doubt, this is my favorite style of all.

While I haven't been to Naples (it is right at the top of places I'd love to visit), it was during a family holiday to another part of Italy where I really started to appreciate what a top-quality Neapolitan pizza looked and tasted like. I vividly remember marveling at the perfectly light and airy crusts, as well as being pleasantly surprised at just how digestible and easy to eat they were.

One of the official regulations set out by the Associazione Verace Pizza Napoletana (AVPN) (an organization founded to uphold the standards of Neapolitan pizza around the world) states that the cooking of a Neapolitan pizza must be done in an oven that has reached 805 to 840°F (430 to 450°C). Step forward all models of the Ooni pizza oven! Whether you are using a model that runs on gas, wood/charcoal or pellets, you will be able to achieve these temperatures in a matter of minutes, meaning you will be cooking a Neapolitan pizza in an incredible 60 to 90 seconds. While I can't claim to follow every single rule set by the AVPN in my pizza making, what I can promise is that I will be detailing every aspect of my process (including plenty of my top tips) to enable you to achieve as close to pizza perfection as possible. It's the small details that make a big difference.

In this chapter, you will find a vast array of Neapolitan pizza recipes, from the simple-but-delicious Underrated Marinara (page 43) to some very unusual recipes involving toppings such as fries (yes, I said fries) and leftover fajitas. One of my favorite pizzas, My Signature Lamb Kofta and Mint Drizzle is in this chapter (page 45), and you can read all about why I designate it as my "signature" pizza and how it was a turning point for me in my quest for pizza perfection.

SUNSHINE MARGHERITA

YIELD: 1 pizza (serves 1–2)

56 g (½ cup) fresh mozzarella

1 (275-g) ball Neapolitan Dough (page 19)

2–3 tbsp (30–45 ml) Keep-It-Simple Tomato Sauce, using canned yellow tomatoes (page 35)

1 tsp finely grated Grana Padano

Drizzle of extra virgin olive oil

Fine semolina flour

Fresh basil leaves

There's no better way to start this chapter than with the iconic Margherita pizza. History tells us that the Margherita pizza was inspired by the three colors (red, white and green) of the Italian flag. It is said to have been named in honor of Queen Margherita of Savoy who, when visiting Naples in 1889, summoned Raffaele Esposito, a local pizza maker, to make her three different pizzas, one being the Margherita. Rather than including the more familiar red version, I decided to go with my yellow Sunshine Margherita! Yellow tomatoes are less acidic than red ones, giving them a slightly sweeter taste. So, if you have a sweet tooth like me, this is the pizza for you! If you're hosting a pizza party, your guests will always expect a Margherita, but for a bit of fun, don't tell them you are using yellow tomatoes and wait for their reactions when you place it down on the table!

To keep the pizza from getting soggy, remove as much moisture from the fresh mozzarella as possible by breaking it into small pieces and laying them down onto a few layers of paper towels at least 1 hour before cooking. To help draw out even more moisture, lay another paper towel on top as well.

Fire up your Ooni pizza oven, and aim for a stone temperature of 800 to 840°F (430 to 450°C). Depending on the outside temperature, this should take approximately 20 minutes. In the colder months, an extra 10 to 15 minutes might be needed. You can check the stone temperature with an infrared thermometer.

When the stone has reached approximately 750°F (400°C), stretch out the dough ball using the instructions on page 21.

Add the yellow tomato sauce to the center of the base and spread in a circular motion, moving out toward the crust using the back of a spoon. Evenly add the Grana Padano and mozzarella before a drizzle of oil. When making a Margherita, use slightly larger pieces of mozzarella in the center. This helps stop the base from doming during the bake.

Give your chosen pizza peel a light dusting of semolina flour before transferring the dough onto it. You can do this by lying the peel flat alongside the dough, and then, using both hands, gently lift the edge of the dough and slide it onto the peel. This stage can be daunting, but be confident and do it in one smooth, quick movement. After sliding the dough onto the peel, give it a final reshape. If you don't feel confident enough to use this technique, you can place the stretched-out dough straight onto the floured peel after stretching it over your knuckles and top while it is on the peel.

(continued)

SUNSHINE MARGHERITA
(CONTINUED)

When the stone temperature has reached 800 to 840°F (430 to 450°C), give the peel a little shuffle/shake to ensure the dough isn't sticking, and then launch confidently into the middle of your Ooni pizza oven. Do not take your eyes off the pizza, as a few seconds can make a big difference to the overall bake!

After approximately 20 seconds, you will begin to see the crust at the back of the oven start to brown/blister. Warm the metal peel/turning peel in the back of the oven by holding it in the flames for a few seconds. (This will help stop the peel from sticking to the bottom of the pizza.) Then, carefully slide it under the pizza and turn it 180 degrees. When the crust that is now at the back of the oven starts to brown/blister, turn the pizza again, but this time, 90 degrees. Finally, do one last 180-degree turn so that all of the pizza has an even bake. The total cooking time should be 60 to 90 seconds. If the base starts to dome, don't worry, just slide the metal peel/turning peel under the base to release the trapped air.

Remove the pizza from the oven and slide it onto a cooling rack for 1 to 2 minutes before transferring to a display board. Neatly add the fresh basil leaves to the center. Cut into 6 slices and serve hot.

THE UNDERRATED MARINARA

YIELD: 1 pizza (serves 1-2)

1 (275-g) ball Neapolitan Dough (page 19)

3-4 tbsp (45-60 ml) Keep-It-Simple Tomato Sauce (page 35)

1 clove garlic, finely sliced

1 tsp dried oregano, plus more for serving

Fresh basil leaves, soaked in salt water*

Drizzle of extra virgin olive oil

Fine semolina flour

* Soaking the basil leaves in salt water protects them from burning, since they are added before baking.

For this particular recipe, the clue is most definitely in the title! It still baffles me how a pizza with only one main topping can taste so incredible. I'll always remember someone telling me, "There's nowhere to hide when making a marinara," which is why it's so important to use good-quality ingredients. A can of good-quality plum tomatoes will really help elevate this pizza to the next level. Traditionally, the marinara just has oregano and garlic added on top of the sauce, but I like to also add a few basil leaves. Some will argue that this means it isn't a traditional marinara, but I just love the extra flavor profile it brings to the pizza.

Pizzas like the marinara, which are light on toppings, tend to dome up and burn, so use more sauce than normal to weigh down the base during the bake. Don't worry about the pizza being too wet once baked, though, as all Ooni pizza ovens can reach a scorching 930°F (500°C), meaning the excess moisture will burn off.

Fire up your Ooni pizza oven, and aim for a stone temperature of 800 to 840°F (430 to 450°C). Depending on the outside temperature, this should take approximately 20 minutes. In the colder months, an extra 10 to 15 minutes might be needed. You can check the stone temperature with an infrared thermometer.

When the stone has reached approximately 750°F (400°C), stretch out the dough ball using the instructions on page 21.

Add the tomato sauce to the center of the base and spread in a circular motion, moving out toward the crust using the back of your spoon. Try and have a bit extra in the center of the base to help prevent it from doming during the bake. Add the garlic, oregano and basil leaves before a final drizzle of oil.

Give your chosen pizza peel a light dusting of semolina flour before transferring the dough onto it. You can do this by lying the peel flat alongside the dough, and then, using both hands, gently lift the edge of the dough and slide it onto the peel. This stage can be daunting, but be confident and do it in one smooth, quick movement. After sliding the dough onto the peel, give it a final reshape. If you don't feel confident enough to use this technique, you can place the stretched-out dough straight onto the floured peel after stretching it over your knuckles and top while it is on the peel.

(continued)

THE UNDERRATED MARINARA (CONTINUED)

When the stone temperature has reached 800 to 840°F (430 to 450°C), give the peel a little shuffle/shake to ensure the dough isn't sticking, and then launch confidently into the middle of your Ooni pizza oven. Do not take your eyes off the pizza, as a few seconds can make a big difference to the overall bake!

After approximately 20 seconds, you will begin to see the crust at the back of the oven start to brown/blister. Warm the metal peel/turning peel in the back of the oven by holding it in the flames for a few seconds. (This will help stop the peel from sticking to the bottom of the pizza.) Then, carefully slide it under the pizza and turn it 180 degrees. Take extra care when sliding the peel under the pizza and turning for the first time. The extra sauce can make the base a little more delicate at this point. When the crust that is now at the back of the oven starts to brown/blister, turn the pizza again, but this time, 90 degrees. Finally, do one last 180-degree turn so that all of the pizza has an even bake. The total cooking time should be 60 to 90 seconds.

Remove the pizza from the oven and slide it onto a cooling rack for 1 to 2 minutes before transferring to a display board. Add a final sprinkle of dried oregano. Cut into 6 slices and serve hot.

MY SIGNATURE LAMB KOFTA AND MINT DRIZZLE

YIELD: 1 pizza (serves 1-2)

56 g (½ cup) fresh mozzarella

Extra virgin olive oil, as needed

2–3 store-bought lamb kofta kebabs

1 (275-g) ball Neapolitan Dough (page 19)

2–3 tbsp (30–45 ml) Keep-It-Simple Tomato Sauce (page 35)

1 tsp finely grated Grana Padano

Fine semolina flour

Drizzle of yogurt mint sauce

Handful of fresh mint, chopped

The pizza that "put me on the map!" A very proud moment early on in my pizza journey was when Ooni asked if they could include this pizza in their Father's Day recipe book. If I remember correctly, "A MILLION-PERCENT YES!" was my response. Just when I thought it couldn't get any better, they then used my photo on the front cover! It was at this point that I started thinking I was actually getting quite good at this pizza making thing. Lamb and mint together is one of the most iconic flavor pairings, which in my opinion, works so well in any dish. Using them on a pizza with fresh mozzarella and tomato sauce is no exception. Lamb kofta is a family favorite and something we eat together on a regular basis, so it was always going to feature on one of my pizzas, and I'm so excited to be able to share it with you.

To keep the pizza from getting soggy, remove as much moisture from the fresh mozzarella as possible by breaking it into small pieces and laying them down onto a few layers of paper towels at least 1 hour before cooking. To help draw out even more moisture, lay another paper towel on top as well.

Fire up your Ooni pizza oven, and aim for a stone temperature of 800 to 840°F (430 to 450°C). Depending on the outside temperature, this should take approximately 20 minutes. In the colder months, an extra 10 to 15 minutes might be needed. You can check the stone temperature with an infrared thermometer.

When the stone temperature of the oven reaches approximately 570°F (300°C), place a cast-iron skillet with a little oil into the oven and let it heat up for 2 minutes. Using your heatproof oven gloves, remove the skillet and add the lamb kofta kebabs. Cook in the oven for 6 to 8 minutes, turning the kebabs every 1 to 2 minutes for a nice, even cook. Remove from the oven, and break the lamb into small pieces. Set aside.

When the stone has reached approximately 750°F (400°C), stretch out the dough ball using the instructions on page 21.

Add the tomato sauce to the center of the base and spread in a circular motion, moving out toward the crust using the back of your spoon. Evenly add the Grana Padano, fresh mozzarella and lamb kofta pieces before a drizzle of oil.

(continued)

MY SIGNATURE LAMB KOFTA AND MINT DRIZZLE (CONTINUED)

Give your chosen pizza peel a light dusting of semolina flour before transferring the dough onto it. You can do this by lying the peel flat alongside the dough, and then, using both hands, gently lift the edge of the dough and slide it onto the peel. This stage can be daunting, but be confident and do it in one smooth, quick movement. After sliding the dough onto the peel, give it a final reshape. If you don't feel confident enough to use this technique, you can place the stretched-out dough straight onto the floured peel after stretching it over your knuckles and top while it is on the peel.

When the stone temperature has reached 800 to 840°F (430 to 450°C), give the peel a little shuffle/shake to ensure the dough isn't sticking, and then launch confidently into the middle of your Ooni pizza oven. Do not take your eyes off the pizza, as a few seconds can make a big difference to the overall bake!

After approximately 20 seconds, you will begin to see the crust at the back of the oven start to brown/blister. Warm the metal peel/turning peel in the back of the oven by holding it in the flames for a few seconds. (This will help stop the peel from sticking to the bottom of the pizza.) Then, carefully slide it under the pizza and turn it 180 degrees. When the crust that is now at the back of the oven starts to brown/blister, turn the pizza again, but this time, 90 degrees. Finally, do one last 180 degree turn so that all of the pizza has an even bake. The total cooking time should be 60 to 90 seconds.

Remove the pizza from the oven and slide it onto a cooling rack for 1 to 2 minutes before transferring to a display board. Add a drizzle of the yogurt mint sauce (I like to do this in a nice and neat zig-zag pattern) before finishing off with a sprinkle of freshy chopped mint leaves. Cut into 6 slices and serve hot.

SMOKY CARB ON CARB

YIELD: 1 pizza (serves 1-2)

For the Roast Potatoes

2 tbsp (30 ml) vegetable oil

1-2 potatoes, peeled and chopped

Salt and pepper, as desired

For the Pizza

1 Italian sausage

Extra virgin olive oil, for frying, plus extra

1 (275-g) ball Neapolitan Dough (page 19)

56 g (½ cup) chopped smoked scamorza

Fresh basil leaves, soaked in salt water*

Fine semolina flour

Drizzle of garlic oil

* Soaking the basil leaves in salt water protects them from burning, since they are added before baking.

In this recipe, I use a cheese called scamorza in place of mozzarella. Scamorza is an Italian cheese that is smoked over beechwood shavings giving it a subtle, smoky flavor. It has a texture comparable to a firm, dry mozzarella, and its flavor works perfectly for a white-based (bianca) pizza alongside fried Italian sausage and roast potatoes. With a low moisture content, scamorza has excellent melting qualities, making it a perfect cheese to use in a hot Ooni pizza oven (up to 930°F [500°C]). If you can't find scamorza, fresh mozzarella can be used as a substitute. With all my recipes, I try to add extra unique touches to make them stand out. Drizzling a bit of garlic oil on this pizza right after it comes out of the oven marries all of these beautiful flavors together.

Preheat your home oven to 400°F (200°C).

I recommend making the roast potatoes the day before and keeping them in the fridge. Add the oil to a roasting tray, and place the tray in the oven to heat up. While heating up, boil the potatoes for 4 to 5 minutes, and then drain them in a colander or sieve. As these are small, do not shake them or they will break up and lose their shape. Carefully remove the hot roasting tray from the oven and place the potatoes on it. Using a spatula, turn the potatoes over in the oil so they are well coated, and season with salt and pepper before roasting for 25 to 30 minutes. It's important not to cook the potatoes for too long as they will be added to the pizza pre-bake and cooked further in the Ooni pizza oven. Set aside.

Fire up your Ooni pizza oven, and aim for a stone temperature of 800 to 840°F (430 to 450°C). Depending on the outside temperature, this should take approximately 20 minutes. In the colder months, an additional 10 to 15 minutes might be needed. You can check the stone temperature with an infrared thermometer.

Remove the sausage from its skin and break it into small pieces. Wet your fingers with water to prevent the sausage meat from sticking to your hands. Gently fry the pieces of sausage in a frying pan over medium heat in a little extra virgin olive oil for 2 to 3 minutes, or until they start to brown. Once cooked, remove the meat from the pan and allow it to cool.

When the stone temperature has reached approximately 750°F (400°C), stretch out the dough ball using the instructions on page 21.

(continued)

SMOKY CARB ON CARB (CONTINUED)

Add the scamorza evenly to the base, making sure not to leave any big gaps. Next, add the basil, sausage meat and roast potatoes before a drizzle of oil. It is important to leave the roast potatoes in the fridge right up until this point as using them cold will help prevent them charring too much under the flames.

Give your chosen pizza peel a light dusting of semolina flour before transferring the dough onto it. You can do this by lying the peel flat alongside the dough, and then, using both hands, gently lift the edge of the dough and slide it onto the peel. This stage can be daunting, but be confident and do it in one smooth, quick movement. After sliding the dough onto the peel, give it a final reshape. If you don't feel confident enough to use this technique, you can place the stretched-out dough straight onto the floured peel after stretching it over your knuckles and top while it is on the peel.

When the stone temperature has reached 800 to 840°F (430 to 450°C), give the peel a little shuffle/shake to ensure the dough isn't sticking and then launch confidently into the middle of your Ooni pizza oven. Do not take your eyes off the pizza, as a few seconds can make a big difference to the overall bake!

After approximately 20 seconds, you will begin to see the crust at the back of the oven start to brown/blister. Warm the metal peel/turning peel in the back of the oven by holding it in the flames for a few seconds. (This will help stop the peel from sticking to the bottom of the pizza.) Then, carefully slide it under the pizza and turn it 180 degrees. When the crust that is now at the back of the oven starts to brown/blister, turn the pizza again, but this time, 90 degrees. Finally, do one last 180-degree turn so that all of the pizza has an even bake. The total cooking time should be 60 to 90 seconds.

Remove the pizza from the oven and slide onto a cooling rack for 1 to 2 minutes before transferring to a display board. Add a drizzle of garlic oil, cut into 6 slices and serve hot.

HOT AND CREAMY 'NDUJA

YIELD: 1 pizza (serves 1-2)

56 g (½ cup) fresh mozzarella

1 (275-g) ball Neapolitan Dough (page 19)

2–3 tbsp (30–45 ml) Keep-It-Simple Tomato Sauce (page 35)

1 tsp finely grated Grana Padano

Fresh basil leaves, soaked in salt water*

15 g 'nduja, broken into small pieces

Drizzle of extra virgin olive oil

Fine semolina flour

1 burrata ball

1 tsp crushed red pepper flakes

* Soaking the basil leaves in salt water protects them from burning, since they are added before baking.

"What is 'nduja?" It is a spicy, spreadable sausage from southern Italy made from a mix of pork, herbs and spices including a generous hit of Calabrian peppers. Before embarking on my pizza journey, I had never heard of 'nduja before, but after the first bite, I remember thinking, *Where have you been all of my life?* It is now one of my favorite toppings. It is becoming more readily available in supermarkets due to its rise in popularity, but, if you can't find it, chorizo is a good alternative. Eaten in its raw form, 'nduja is seriously HOT, but when used on a pizza alongside tomato sauce and mozzarella cheese, this heat is mellowed slightly, making for a much more pleasant eating experience. Add in some dollops of smooth and creamy Burrata cheese with a sprinkle of crushed red pepper flakes and you will be in pizza heaven.

To keep the pizza from getting soggy, remove as much moisture from the fresh mozzarella as possible by breaking it into small pieces and laying them down onto a few layers of paper towels at least 1 hour before cooking. To help draw out even more moisture, lay another paper towel on top as well.

Fire up your Ooni pizza oven, and aim for a stone temperature of 800 to 840°F (430 to 450°C). Depending on the outside temperature, this should take approximately 20 minutes. In the colder months, an extra 10 to 15 minutes might be needed. You can check the stone temperature with an infrared thermometer.

When the stone has reached approximately 750°F (400°C), stretch out the dough ball using the instructions on page 21.

Add the tomato sauce to the center of the base and spread in a circular motion, moving out toward the crust using the back of a spoon. Evenly add the Grana Padano, basil leaves, fresh mozzarella and pieces of 'nduja before a drizzle of oil.

Give your chosen pizza peel a light dusting of semolina flour before transferring the dough onto it. You can do this by lying the peel flat alongside the dough, and then, using both hands, gently lift the edge of the dough and slide it onto the peel. This stage can be daunting, but be confident and do it in one smooth, quick movement. After sliding the dough onto the peel, give it a final reshape. If you don't feel confident enough to use this technique, you can place the stretched-out dough straight onto the floured peel after stretching it over your knuckles and top while it is on the peel.

(continued)

HOT AND CREAMY 'NDUJA (CONTINUED)

When the stone temperature has reached 800 to 840°F (430 to 450°C), give the peel a little shuffle/shake to ensure the dough isn't sticking, and then launch confidently into the middle of your Ooni pizza oven. Do not take your eyes off the pizza, as a few seconds can make a big difference to the overall bake!

After approximately 20 seconds, you will begin to see the crust at the back of the oven start to brown/blister. Warm the metal peel/turning peel in the back of the oven by holding it in the flames for a few seconds. (This will help stop the peel from sticking to the bottom of the pizza.) Then, carefully slide it under the pizza and turn it 180 degrees. When the crust that is now at the back of the oven starts to brown/blister, turn the pizza again, but this time, 90 degrees. Finally, do one last 180-degree turn so that all of the pizza has an even bake. The total cooking time should be 60 to 90 seconds.

Remove the pizza from the oven and slide onto a cooling rack for 1 to 2 minutes before transferring to a display board. Add some dollops of the burrata between the pieces of 'nduja before adding a sprinkle of red pepper flakes. As the burrata has an outer casing/skin, I like to open the casing and squeeze out the soft creamy center into a bowl before using a spoon to add it to the pizza. Cut into 6 slices and serve hot.

CHEESY GARLIC BREAD PIZZA WITH A TWIST

YIELD: 1 pizza (serves 1-2)

For the Garlic and Herb Butter

2 tbsp (28 g) softened salted butter

2 cloves garlic, crushed or finely chopped

1 tsp dried parsley or rosemary

For the Pizza

56 g (½ cup) fresh mozzarella

1 (275-g) ball Neapolitan Dough (page 19)

56 g (½ cup) grated low-moisture mozzarella

Fine semolina flour

¼ tsp dried parsley

Drizzle of balsamic glaze

This pizza is dedicated to my amazing daughter, Lily. For someone so young, she has been incredibly supportive of me, and since making my first ever cheesy garlic bread pizza, this has been her favorite and is definitely the pizza I make most often. I know what you're thinking: Balsamic with cheese and garlic sounds like an unusual combination. (I thought the same when I first saw it.) But trust me, it really does work, and in my opinion, takes this pizza to another level! While it is undoubtedly great to have this on its own as an individual pizza, this is also wonderful as a starter or a sharer with friends or family. A great tip is to make a little extra dough over the weekend so you can create one of these to accompany your midweek pasta dish.

To make the garlic and herb butter, in your mixing bowl, combine the butter, garlic and parsley. This can be made ahead of time and kept in the fridge, but be sure to let it soften before using.

To keep the pizza from getting soggy, remove as much moisture from the fresh mozzarella as possible by breaking it into small pieces and laying them down onto a few layers of paper towels at least 1 hour before cooking. To help draw out even more moisture, lay another paper towel on top as well.

Fire up your Ooni pizza oven, and aim for a stone temperature of 800 to 840°F (430 to 450°C). Depending on the outside temperature, this should take approximately 20 minutes. In the colder months, an extra 10 to 15 minutes might be needed. You can check the stone temperature with an infrared thermometer.

When the stone has reached approximately 750°F (400°C), stretch out the dough ball using the instructions on page 21.

With the back of a spoon, spread the garlic and herb butter onto the base so it has a nice, even layer all the way up to where the crust starts. Sprinkle the grated mozzarella onto the garlic and herb butter before adding the pieces of fresh mozzarella.

(continued)

CHEESY GARLIC BREAD PIZZA WITH A TWIST (CONTINUED)

Give your chosen pizza peel a light dusting of semolina flour before transferring the dough onto it. You can do this by lying the peel flat alongside the dough, and then, using both hands, gently lift the edge of the dough and slide it onto the peel. This stage can be daunting, but be confident and do it in one smooth, quick movement. After sliding the dough onto the peel, give it a final reshape. If you don't feel confident enough to use this technique, you can place the stretched-out dough straight onto the floured peel after stretching it over your knuckles and top while it is on the peel.

When the stone temperature has reached 800 to 840°F (430 to 450°C), give the peel a little shuffle/shake to ensure the dough isn't sticking, and then launch confidently into the middle of your Ooni pizza oven. Do not take your eyes off the pizza, as a few seconds can make a big difference to the overall bake!

After approximately 20 seconds, you will begin to see the crust at the back of the oven start to brown/blister. Warm the metal peel/turning peel in the back of the oven by holding it in the flames for a few seconds. (This will help stop the peel from sticking to the bottom of the pizza.) Then, carefully slide it under the pizza and turn it 180 degrees. When the crust that is now at the back of the oven starts to brown/blister, turn the pizza again, but this time, 90 degrees. Finally, do one last 180-degree turn so that all of the pizza has an even bake. The total cooking time should be 60 to 90 seconds.

Remove the pizza from the oven and slide onto a cooling rack for 1 to 2 minutes before transferring to a display board. Add a sprinkle of parsley and a drizzle of balsamic glaze to finish. Cut into 6 slices and serve hot.

FAJITA FIESTA PIZZA

YIELD: 1 pizza (serves 1-2)

For the Fajita Toppings
1 tsp vegetable oil

60 g chicken, cut into small pieces

75 g (½ cup) chopped peppers

1 tbsp (7 g) fajita seasoning

For the Pizza
56 g (½ cup) fresh mozzarella

1 (275-g) ball Neapolitan Dough (page 19)

2 tbsp (30 ml) tomato salsa

1 small red onion, sliced into circles

Drizzle of extra virgin olive oil

Fine semolina flour

1 tbsp (15 ml) sour cream

1 tbsp (14 g) guacamole

This pizza is dedicated to my wife, Nikki, who not only took the incredible photos in this book, but is also responsible for coming up with the idea for this pizza. Fajitas are a meal that we have as a family most weeks, and we always look forward to Fajita Friday (though not quite as much as Pizza Sunday). This recipe was born around the dinner table one Friday evening. Adding gooey cheese and a lovely soft pizza dough to the spicy fajita flavors is a match made in the Ooni! Rather than making the toppings from scratch, have fajitas the night before, and make a little extra to use on this pizza. Storing the fajita-spiced chicken and peppers overnight in the fridge will intensify the flavors.

If you don't have fajita leftovers, cook your fajita toppings while your Ooni pizza oven is heating up. In a wok or frying pan, heat the vegetable oil over a medium heat, and then add the chicken and fry until cooked through. Add the peppers and the fajita seasoning and toss together so they are all evenly coated. When the peppers start to soften, remove them and the chicken from the wok and allow them to cool. (You can add the red onion at this stage, but I like to add them to the pizza raw later in the recipe to maintain that nice vibrant color.) Set aside while you prep your other pizza toppings and dough.

To keep the pizza from getting soggy, remove as much moisture from the fresh mozzarella as possible by breaking it into small pieces and laying them down onto a few layers of paper towels at least 1 hour before cooking. To help draw out even more moisture, lay another paper towel on top as well.

Fire up your Ooni pizza oven, and aim for a stone temperature of 800 to 840°F (430 to 450°C). Depending on the outside temperature, this should take approximately 20 minutes. In the colder months, an extra 10 to 15 minutes might be needed. You can check the stone temperature with an infrared thermometer.

When the stone has reached approximately 750°F (400°C), stretch out the dough ball using the instructions on page 21.

Add the tomato salsa to the center of the base and spread in a circular motion, moving out toward the crust using the back of your spoon. Evenly add the mozzarella, chicken and peppers and red onion before a drizzle of oil.

(continued)

FAJITA FIESTA PIZZA (CONTINUED)

Give your chosen pizza peel a light dusting of semolina flour before transferring the dough onto it. You can do this by laying the peel flat alongside the dough, and then, using both hands, gently lifting the edge of the dough and sliding it onto the peel. This stage can be daunting, but be confident and do it in one smooth, quick movement. After sliding the dough onto the peel, give it a final reshape. If you don't feel confident enough to use this technique, you can place the stretched-out dough straight onto the floured peel after stretching it over your knuckles and top while it is on the peel.

When the stone temperature has reached 800 to 840°F (430 to 450°C), give the peel a little shuffle/shake to ensure the dough isn't sticking, and then launch confidently into the middle of your Ooni pizza oven. Do not take your eyes off the pizza, as a few seconds can make a big difference to the overall bake!

After approximately 20 seconds, you will begin to see the crust at the back of the oven start to brown/blister. Warm the metal peel/turning peel in the back of the oven by holding it in the flames for a few seconds. (This will help stop the peel from sticking to the bottom of the pizza.) Then, carefully slide it under the pizza and turn it 180 degrees. When the crust that is now at the back of the oven starts to brown/blister, turn the pizza again, but this time, 90 degrees. Finally, do one last 180-degree turn so that all of the pizza has an even bake. The total cooking time should be 60 to 90 seconds.

Remove the pizza from the oven and slide onto a cooling rack for 1 to 2 minutes before transferring to a display board. Add small dollops of sour cream and guacamole evenly around the pizza to finish. Cut into 6 slices and serve hot.

FIG, PROSCIUTTO ... AND A WHOLE LOT MORE!

YIELD: 1 pizza (serves 1-2)

56 g (½ cup) fresh mozzarella

1 (275-g) ball Neapolitan Dough (page 19)

2-3 tbsp (30-45 ml) Keep-It-Simple Tomato Sauce (page 35)

10 g blue cheese, chopped into small pieces

2-3 prosciutto slices

2 figs, cut into thin wedges

Drizzle of extra virgin olive oil

Fine semolina flour

Fresh rocket

1 tbsp (9 g) chopped toasted almonds

Grana Padano shavings

Drizzle of balsamic glaze

Figs pair notoriously well with nuts, prosciutto and cheese, so my thought process behind this recipe was: *Why not use them all together?* The result was a beautiful marriage of flavors and texture that will have your taste buds tingling. A key element to get right with this recipe is the choice of blue cheese. To make sure you don't overpower the other flavors, my advice is to choose a creamy variety, as these have better melting properties and a mellower flavor, which will work superbly with the sweet figs and acidic balsamic glaze. Toasting the almonds might seem like an extra effort, but by doing so, they will become crunchier, and their flavor will be enhanced. Making additional efforts like this will help elevate your pizzas to new levels, and give them that "wow" factor we all strive to achieve.

To keep the pizza from getting soggy, remove as much moisture from the fresh mozzarella as possible by breaking it into small pieces and laying them down onto a few layers of paper towels at least 1 hour before cooking. To help draw out even more moisture, lay another paper towel on top as well.

Fire up your Ooni pizza oven, and aim for a stone temperature of 800 to 840°F (430 to 450°C). Depending on the outside temperature, this should take approximately 20 minutes. In the colder months, an extra 10 to 15 minutes might be needed. You can check the stone temperature with an infrared thermometer.

When the stone has reached approximately 750°F (400°C), stretch out the dough ball using the instructions on page 21.

Add the tomato sauce to the center of the base and spread in a circular motion, moving out toward the crust using the back of your spoon. Next, evenly add the mozzarella, blue cheese, prosciutto and figs before a drizzle of oil. To ensure the prosciutto crisps up in the oven, crinkle the pieces slightly when adding to the base. As the blue cheese is a powerful flavor, my tip is to use very small pieces evenly distributed to avoid overpowering the rest of the toppings.

Give your chosen pizza peel a light dusting of semolina flour before transferring the dough onto it. Due to the fig wedges, this pizza is heavier than normal, meaning it can be a little trickier to maintain the round shape of the pizza during the launch. To help with this, you can use a little bit more semolina flour on your peel. You can transfer the dough by lying the peel flat alongside the dough, and then, using both hands, gently lift the edge of the dough and slide it onto the peel. This stage can be daunting, but be confident and do it in one smooth, quick movement. After sliding the dough onto the peel, give it a final reshape.

(continued)

FIG, PROSCIUTTO ...
AND A WHOLE
LOT MORE!
(CONTINUED)

If you don't feel confident enough to use this technique, you can place the stretched-out dough straight onto the floured peel after stretching it over your knuckles and top while it is on the peel.

When the stone temperature has reached 800 to 840°F (430 to 450°C), give the peel a little shuffle/shake to ensure the dough isn't sticking, and then launch confidently into the middle of your Ooni pizza oven. Do not take your eyes off the pizza, as a few seconds can make a big difference to the overall bake!

After approximately 20 seconds, you will begin to see the crust at the back of the oven start to brown/blister. Warm the metal peel/turning peel in the back of the oven by holding it in the flames for a few seconds. (This will help stop the peel from sticking to the bottom of the pizza.) Then, carefully slide it under the pizza and turn it 180 degrees. When the crust that is now at the back of the oven starts to brown/blister, turn the pizza again, but this time, 90 degrees. Finally, do one last 180-degree turn so that all of the pizza has an even bake. The total cooking time should be 60 to 90 seconds.

Remove the pizza from the oven and slide it onto a cooling rack for 1 to 2 minutes before transferring to a display board. Add the fresh rocket, chopped almonds and Grana Padano shavings before a drizzle of balsamic glaze to finish. Cut into 6 slices and serve hot.

MEXICAN STREET CORN (ELOTE) PIZZA

YIELD: 1 pizza (serves 1-2)

For the Elote Sauce

2 tbsp (30 ml) mayonnaise

1 tbsp (15 ml) sour cream

¼ tsp paprika

¼ tsp chili powder

For the Pizza

56 g (½ cup) fresh mozzarella

1 corncob

½ tbsp (7 g) butter

Squeeze of lime juice

1 (275-g) ball Neapolitan Dough (page 19)

Drizzle of extra virgin olive oil

Fine semolina flour

10 g cotija or feta cheese, crumbled

1 tsp crushed red pepper flakes

Handful of chopped coriander or cilantro

Elote is an authentic Mexican corn on the cob commonly sold by *eloteros* on street corners throughout Mexico. After being cooked, the cobs are coated in a Mexican crema or mayonnaise and lime juice, and then rolled in crumbled cotija cheese and sprinkled with chili powder. While researching this before making my first elote pizza, I continuously came across the words, "the only way you should ever eat corn." This was enough to convince me that I needed to get these flavors onto a pizza. Why not host a Mexican-themed pizza party serving this alongside my Fajita Fiesta Pizza (page 57), all washed down with some refreshing margaritas?

To make your elote sauce, add the mayonnaise, sour cream, paprika and chili powder to a bowl and stir until combined. Set aside.

To keep the pizza from getting soggy, remove as much moisture from the fresh mozzarella as possible by breaking it into small pieces and laying them down onto a few layers of paper towels at least 1 hour before cooking. To help draw out even more moisture, lay another paper towel on top as well.

Fire up your Ooni pizza oven, and aim for a stone temperature of 800 to 840°F (430 to 450°C). Depending on the outside temperature, this should take approximately 20 minutes. In the colder months, an extra 10 to 15 minutes might be needed. You can check the stone temperature with an infrared thermometer.

While your Ooni pizza oven is heating up, preheat your home oven grill/broiler. Remove the husk of your corncob, if necessary, and place it on a baking tray. Spread the butter over the corn and squeeze over the lime juice. Cook for 8 to 10 minutes (turning regularly) until the kernels start to darken. Stand the corn up, and using a sharp knife cut the kernels off, from top to bottom. I like to try and keep clusters of the kernels together, as I think it gives the finished pizza a nice look.

When the stone has reached approximately 750°F (400°C), stretch out the dough ball using the instructions on page 21.

Add 2 to 3 tablespoons (30–45 ml) of the elote sauce to the center of the base and spread in a circular motion, moving out toward the crust using the back of your spoon. Next, evenly add the mozzarella and grilled corn before a drizzle of oil. If like me you have kept clusters of the corn together, be careful when adding them to the pizza as they are very delicate and can break apart very easily.

(continued)

MEXICAN STREET CORN (ELOTE) PIZZA (CONTINUED)

Give your chosen pizza peel a light dusting of semolina flour before transferring the dough onto it. You can do this by lying the peel flat alongside the dough, and then, using both hands, gently lift the edge of the dough and slide it onto the peel. This stage can be daunting, but be confident and do it in one smooth, quick movement. After sliding the dough onto the peel, give it a final reshape. If you don't feel confident enough to use this technique, you can place the stretched-out dough straight onto the floured peel after stretching it over your knuckles and top while it is on the peel.

When the stone temperature has reached 800 to 840°F (430 to 450°C), give the peel a little shuffle/shake to ensure the dough isn't sticking, and then launch confidently into the middle of your Ooni pizza oven. Do not take your eyes off the pizza, as a few seconds can make a big difference to the overall bake!

After approximately 20 seconds, you will begin to see the crust at the back of the oven start to brown/blister. Warm the metal peel/turning peel in the back of the oven by holding it in the flames for a few seconds. (This will help stop the peel from sticking to the bottom of the pizza.) Then, carefully slide it under the pizza and turn it 180 degrees. When the crust that is now at the back of the oven starts to brown/blister, turn the pizza again, but this time, 90 degrees. Finally, do one last 180-degree turn so that all of the pizza has an even bake. The total cooking time should be 60 to 90 seconds.

Remove the pizza from the oven and slide it onto a cooling rack for 1 to 2 minutes before transferring to a display board. Evenly sprinkle the crumbled cotija/feta cheese and chili flakes before adding the chopped coriander to finish. Cut into 6 slices and serve hot.

THE FRIDGE RAIDER

YIELD: 1 pizza (serves 1-2)

56 g (½ cup) fresh mozzarella

2-3 tbsp (30-45 ml) Keep-It-Simple Tomato Sauce (page 35)

1 tbsp (15 ml) barbecue sauce

1 tsp (5 ml) vegetable oil

1 clove garlic, crushed or finely chopped

1 handful spinach, washed and dried

1 (275-g) ball Neapolitan Dough (page 19)

1 tsp finely grated Grana Padano

60 g roast chicken, cut into small pieces

17 g sliced jalapeños

1 small red onion, sliced into circles

Drizzle of extra virgin olive oil

Fine semolina flour

1 tbsp (15 ml) sour cream

Drizzle of hot honey

If, like me, you get to the end of the week and your fridge is full of leftovers that are probably going to end up being thrown away, fire up your Ooni pizza oven and make yourself a Fridge Raider! While the ingredients I use work perfectly, this recipe is more about encouraging you to experiment with leftovers. Experimenting is how I have gained most of my knowledge so far, and it's such a great way to learn. This pizza is what introduced me to using barbecue sauce with tomato sauce as a base, and it is now something I use all the time. Without raiding my fridge that day, I would not have stumbled across this beautiful flavor.

I dedicate this pizza to my late grandad "Ernie," who passed on to me many of his wonderful values, one of which was to try and waste as little as possible! At family meals, he would always be finishing off what others had left on their plates just so it wouldn't be thrown away.

To keep the pizza from getting soggy, remove as much moisture from the fresh mozzarella as possible by breaking it into small pieces and laying them down onto a few layers of paper towels at least 1 hour before cooking. To help draw out even more moisture, lay another paper towel on top as well.

In a bowl, mix together the tomato sauce and barbecue sauce. To intensify the flavor, make this the day before and store in the fridge until ready to use. Be sure to let it get back to room temperature before using.

Fire up your Ooni pizza oven, and aim for a stone temperature of 800 to 840°F (430 to 450°C). Depending on the outside temperature, this should take approximately 20 minutes. In the colder months, an extra 10 to 15 minutes might be needed. You can check the stone temperature using an infrared thermometer.

While your Ooni pizza oven is heating up, in a wok or frying pan, heat up the vegetable oil over a medium heat, and add the garlic and spinach. Use kitchen tongs to toss and turn the spinach until it has all wilted. (This should only take 30 to 60 seconds.) Place the spinach (spaced out) onto a plate, and allow it to cool.

When the stone has reached approximately 750°F (400°C), stretch out the dough ball using the instructions on page 21.

Add the barbecue-tomato sauce to the center of the base and spread in a circular motion, moving out toward the crust using the back of your spoon. Next, evenly add the Grana Padano, fresh mozzarella, chicken, spinach, jalapeños and red onion, before a drizzle of oil.

(continued)

THE FRIDGE RAIDER
(CONTINUED)

Give your chosen pizza peel a light dusting of semolina flour before transferring the dough onto it. You can do this by lying the peel flat alongside the dough, and then, using both hands, gently lift the edge of the dough and slide it onto the peel. This stage can be daunting, but be confident and do it in one smooth, quick movement. After sliding the dough onto the peel, give it a final reshape. If you don't feel confident enough to use this technique, you can place the stretched-out dough straight onto the floured peel after stretching it over your knuckles and top while it is on the peel.

When the stone temperature has reached 800 to 840°F (430 to 450°C), give the peel a little shuffle/shake to ensure the dough isn't sticking, and then launch confidently into the middle of your Ooni pizza oven. Do not take your eyes off the pizza, as a few seconds can make a big difference to the overall bake!

After approximately 20 seconds, you will begin to see the crust at the back of the oven start to brown/blister. Warm the metal peel/turning peel in the back of the oven by holding it in the flames for a few seconds. (This will help stop the peel from sticking to the bottom of the pizza.) Then, carefully slide it under the pizza and turn it 180 degrees. When the crust that is now at the back of the oven starts to brown/blister, turn the pizza again, but this time, 90 degrees. Finally, do one last 180-degree turn so that all of the pizza has an even bake. The total cooking time should be 60 to 90 seconds.

Remove the pizza from the oven and slide it onto a cooling rack for 1 to 2 minutes before transferring to a display board. Add small dollops of sour cream evenly around the pizza before adding a generous drizzle of hot honey. Cut into 6 slices and serve hot.

PROSCIUTTO BIANCA

YIELD: 1 pizza (serves 1-2)

74 g (⅔ cup) fresh mozzarella
2 tbsp (28 g) ricotta
½ tsp lemon juice
Pinch of salt
1 (275-g) ball Neapolitan Dough (page 19)
25 g prosciutto
Drizzle of extra virgin olive oil
Fine semolina flour
1 tbsp (16 g) chili jam
Lemon zest, for garnishing

A pizza bianca (white pizza) is made without tomato sauce, and uses one or more varieties of cheese as the base. With most of my white-based pizzas, I like to use ricotta and mozzarella, as I find that the contrast in textures works perfectly together. To give this creamy base a bit of a lift, I add some fresh lemon juice to the ricotta, which gives a subtle background flavor to the whole pizza. Not having the tomato sauce means the pizza will be quite rich and creamy, so I think it's very important to choose wisely when it comes to the toppings. To cut through the richness, I have used small dollops of chili jam post-bake. Prosciutto is a topping I use frequently on pizza, most of the time added post-bake, but with this recipe, I like using it pre-bake. It crisps up brilliantly and gives the pizza a different texture.

To keep the pizza from getting soggy, remove as much moisture from the fresh mozzarella as possible by breaking it into small pieces and laying them down onto a few layers of paper towels at least 1 hour before cooking. To help draw out even more moisture, lay another paper towel on top as well.

Add the ricotta, lemon juice and salt to a bowl. Mix well and set aside.

Fire up your Ooni pizza oven, and aim for a stone temperature of 800 to 840°F (430 to 450°C). Depending on the outside temperature, this should take approximately 20 minutes. In the colder months, an extra 10 to 15 minutes might be needed. You can check the stone temperature with an infrared thermometer.

When the stone has reached approximately 750°F (400°C), stretch out the dough ball using the instructions on page 21.

Add the pieces of fresh mozzarella to the base before adding small dollops of the lemon-infused ricotta. Try to add the ricotta in the small gaps between the pieces of mozzarella to give a nice uniform coverage. Add the prosciutto before a drizzle of oil. To ensure the prosciutto crisps up in the oven, crinkle the pieces slightly when adding to the base.

Give your chosen pizza peel a light dusting of semolina flour before transferring the dough onto it. You can do this by lying the peel flat alongside the dough, and then, using both hands, gently lift the edge of the dough and slide it onto the peel. This stage can be daunting, but be confident and do it in one smooth, quick movement. After sliding the dough onto the peel, give it a final reshape. If you don't feel confident enough to use this technique, you can place the stretched-out dough straight onto the floured peel after stretching it over your knuckles and top while it is on the peel.

(continued)

PROSCIUTTO BIANCA (CONTINUED)

When the stone temperature has reached 800 to 840°F (430 to 450°C), give the peel a little shuffle/shake to ensure the dough isn't sticking, and then launch confidently into the middle of your Ooni pizza oven. Do not take your eyes off the pizza, as a few seconds can make a big difference to the overall bake!

After approximately 20 seconds, you will begin to see the crust at the back of the oven start to brown/blister. Warm the metal peel/turning peel in the back of the oven by holding it in the flames for a few seconds. (This will help stop the peel from sticking to the bottom of the pizza.) Then, carefully slide it under the pizza and turn it 180 degrees. When the crust that is now at the back of the oven starts to brown/blister, turn the pizza again, but this time, 90 degrees. Finally, do one last 180-degree turn so that all of the pizza has an even bake. The total cooking time should be 60 to 90 seconds.

Remove the pizza from the oven and slide it onto a cooling rack for 1 to 2 minutes before transferring to a display board. Add small dollops of chili jam evenly around the pizza. The key here is to make sure there is enough jam so that each bite has a bit of that chili kick! Grate some fresh lemon zest all over the pizza to finish. Cut into 6 slices and serve hot.

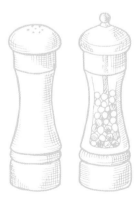

A SLICE OF INDIA

YIELD: 1 pizza (serves 1-2)

For the Roast Potatoes

1-2 small roasting potatoes, peeled and chopped

2 tbsp (30 ml) vegetable oil

½ tsp curry powder

Salt and pepper, as desired

For the Pizza

56 g (½ cup) fresh mozzarella

2-3 tbsp (30-45 ml) Keep-It-Simple Tomato Sauce (page 35)

¼ tsp chili powder

¼ tsp curry powder

1 (275-g) ball Neapolitan Dough (page 19)

50 g store-bought chicken tikka, cut into small pieces

Drizzle of extra virgin olive oil

Fine semolina flour

1 store-bought poppadom, broken into small pieces

Drizzle of yogurt mint sauce

2 tsp (10 ml) mango chutney

Handful of chopped coriander or cilantro

When I first made this pizza, I was very skeptical as to whether it was going to be a success or not. As I'm sure you can guess from the fact that it has made it into this book, it was a roaring success and is actually one of the best pizzas I have ever made! I've seen and tasted a few different Indian-inspired pizzas, but there are certain aspects of this recipe that elevate it above the rest, in my opinion. Adding spices to my Keep-It-Simple Tomato Sauce (page 35) and adding poppadoms with mango chutney post-bake makes this a pizza you will want to make over and over again. I love using potato on pizza; I think it works so well, especially mini roast potatoes. With the flames in Ooni pizza ovens being so fierce, the edges and corners of the potatoes will catch and char slightly, giving a beautiful extra flavor to this already appetizing pizza.

Preheat your home oven to 400°F (200°C).

I recommend making the curried roast potatoes the day before and keeping them in the fridge. Add the oil to a roasting tray, and place the tray in the oven to heat up. While heating up, boil the potatoes for 4 to 5 minutes, and then drain them in a colander or sieve. As these are small, do not shake them or they will break up and lose their shape. Carefully remove the hot roasting tray from the oven and place the potatoes on it. Sprinkle the curry powder evenly over the potatoes. Using a spatula, turn the potatoes over in the oil so they are well coated, and season with salt and pepper before roasting for 25 to 30 minutes. It's important not to cook the potatoes for too long as they will be added to the pizza pre-bake and cooked further in Ooni pizza oven. Set aside.

To keep the pizza from getting soggy, remove as much moisture from the fresh mozzarella as possible by breaking it into small pieces and laying them down onto a few layers of paper towels at least 1 hour before cooking. To help draw out even more moisture, lay another paper towel on top as well.

In a bowl, add the tomato sauce, chili powder and curry powder and mix thoroughly. To intensify the flavor, make this the day before and store in the fridge. Be sure to let it get to room temperature before using.

Fire up your Ooni pizza oven, and aim for a stone temperature of 800 to 840°F (430 to 450°C). Depending on the outside temperature, this should take approximately 20 minutes. In the colder months, an extra 10 to 15 minutes might be needed. You can check the stone temperature with an infrared thermometer.

(continued)

A SLICE OF INDIA (CONTINUED)

When the stone has reached approximately 750°F (400°C), stretch out the dough ball using the instructions on page 21.

Add the spicy tomato sauce to the center of the base and spread in a circular motion, moving out toward the crust using the back of your spoon. Next, evenly add the fresh mozzarella, chicken tikka pieces and curried roast potatoes before a drizzle of oil. It is important to leave the curried roast potatoes in the fridge right up until this point as using them cold will help prevent them charring too much under the flames in your Ooni pizza oven.

Give your chosen pizza peel a light dusting of semolina flour before transferring the dough onto it. You can do this by lying the peel flat alongside the dough, and then, using both hands, gently lift the edge of the dough and slide it onto the peel. This stage can be daunting, but be confident and do it in one smooth, quick movement. After sliding the dough onto the peel, give it a final reshape. If you don't feel confident enough to use this technique, you can place the stretched-out dough straight onto the floured peel after stretching it over your knuckles and top while it is on the peel.

When the stone temperature has reached 800 to 840°F (430 to 450°C), give the peel a little shuffle/shake to ensure the dough isn't sticking, and then launch confidently into the middle of your Ooni pizza oven. Do not take your eyes off the pizza, as a few seconds can make a big difference to the overall bake!

After approximately 20 seconds, you will begin to see the crust at the back of the oven start to brown/blister. Warm the metal peel/turning peel in the back of the oven by holding it in the flames for a few seconds. (This will help stop the peel from sticking to the bottom of the pizza.) Then, carefully slide it under the pizza and turn it 180 degrees. When the crust that is now at the back of the oven starts to brown/blister, turn the pizza again, but this time, 90 degrees. Finally, do one last 180-degree turn so that all of the pizza has an even bake. The total cooking time should be 60 to 90 seconds.

Remove the pizza from the oven and slide it onto a cooling rack for 1 to 2 minutes before transferring to a display board. Evenly add the pieces of poppadom and small dollops of the yogurt mint sauce and mango chutney. Try to add these into all the small gaps in the rest of the toppings so that you get all these wonderful flavors with every bite. Add the chopped coriander. Cut into 6 slices and serve hot.

WINNER, WINNER, CHICKEN ... BURGER PIZZA

YIELD: 1 pizza (serves 1-2)

56 g (½ cup) fresh mozzarella

1-2 slices smoky bacon

30 g chorizo, cut into small cubes

1 (275-g) ball Neapolitan Dough (page 19)

2-3 tbsp (30-45 ml) Keep-It-Simple Tomato Sauce (page 35)

1 tsp finely grated Grana Padano

70 g roast chicken, cut into small pieces

10 g Cheddar cheese

Drizzle of extra virgin olive oil

Fine semolina flour

1 tbsp (16 g) chili jam

Handful of chopped coriander or cilantro

I'm a big advocate of "less is more" when it comes to topping a Neapolitan pizza, but sometimes I throw the rule book out the window and go a bit wild! I have found that inspiration for recipes and topping combinations can come when you least expect it, from absolutely anywhere. This recipe was inspired by a visit to a local restaurant where I noticed an interesting-sounding chicken, bacon, chorizo and chili jam burger on the menu. Whoever was responsible for creating that burger certainly understood flavor, because all these toppings complement each other perfectly. Using several varieties of cheese does make it quite creamy, but this is offset nicely by the chorizo and chili jam.

To keep the pizza from getting soggy, remove as much moisture from the fresh mozzarella as possible by breaking it into small pieces and laying them down onto a few layers of paper towels at least 1 hour before cooking. To help draw out even more moisture, lay another paper towel on top as well.

Fire up your Ooni pizza oven, and aim for a stone temperature of 800 to 840°F (430 to 450°C). Depending on the outside temperature, this should take approximately 20 minutes. In the colder months, an extra 10 to 15 minutes might be needed. You can check the stone temperature with an infrared thermometer.

While your Ooni pizza oven is heating up, fry the bacon in a frying pan until it starts to brown and crisp. It's important not to cook the bacon for too long as it will be added to the pizza pre-bake and cooked further in your Ooni pizza oven. Cut the bacon into small pieces. To add an extra flavor element into this pizza, put the chopped chorizo into the hot frying pan and rendered bacon fat and cook (tossing regularly) for 1 to 2 minutes.

When the stone has reached approximately 750°F (400°C), stretch out the dough ball using the instructions on page 21.

Add the tomato sauce to the center of the base and spread in a circular motion, moving out toward the crust using the back of your spoon. Next, evenly add the Grana Padano, fresh mozzarella, roast chicken, Cheddar cheese, smoky bacon and chorizo before a drizzle of oil.

(continued)

WINNER, WINNER, CHICKEN . . . BURGER PIZZA (CONTINUED)

Give your chosen pizza peel a light dusting of semolina flour before transferring the dough onto it. You can do this by lying the peel flat alongside the dough, and then, using both hands, gently lifting the edge of the dough and sliding it onto the peel. This stage can be daunting, but be confident and do it in one smooth, quick movement. After sliding the dough onto the peel, give it a final reshape. If you don't feel confident enough to use this technique, you can place the stretched-out dough straight onto the floured peel after stretching it over your knuckles and top while it is on the peel.

When the stone temperature has reached 800 to 840°F (430 to 450°C), give the peel a little shuffle/shake to ensure the dough isn't sticking, and then launch confidently into the middle of your Ooni pizza oven. Do not take your eyes off the pizza, as a few seconds can make a big difference to the overall bake!

After approximately 20 seconds, you will begin to see the crust at the back of the oven start to brown/blister. Warm the metal peel/turning peel in the back of the oven by holding it in the flames for a few seconds. (This will help stop the peel from sticking to the bottom of the pizza.) Then, carefully slide it under the pizza and turn it 180 degrees. When the crust that is now at the back of the oven starts to brown/blister, turn the pizza again, but this time, 90 degrees. Finally, do one last 180-degree turn so that all of the pizza has an even bake. The total cooking time should be 60 to 90 seconds.

Remove the pizza from the oven and slide it onto a cooling rack for 1 to 2 minutes before transferring to a display board. Add small dollops of chili jam evenly around the pizza. The key here is to make sure there is enough chili jam so that each bite has a bit of that chili kick! Add the chopped coriander. Cut into 6 slices and serve hot.

HOT DIGGITY DOG PIZZA

YIELD: 1 pizza (serves 1-2)

56 g (½ cup) fresh mozzarella

1 hot dog or standard sausage

1 (275-g) ball Neapolitan Dough (page 19)

2–3 tbsp (30–45 ml) Keep-It-Simple Tomato Sauce (page 35)

1 tsp finely grated Grana Padano

Drizzle of extra virgin olive oil

Fine semolina flour

Drizzle of yellow mustard

Handful of store-bought crispy onions

If you love hot dogs and you love pizza, then this is definitely the pizza for you! I first saw a hot-dog inspired pizza made by one of my fellow Ooni ambassadors, Lewis Pope (aka Unholy Pizza), so I have him to thank for bringing this pizza into my life. I have always been a big fan of hot dogs; they bring back lovely childhood memories of an annual Scouts' bonfire night where we would all sit around the bonfire eating hot dogs while eagerly awaiting the start of the fireworks. For this recipe, you can use hot dog (frankfurter) sausages or normal sausages; both work extremely well. I love recreating some of my favorite dishes in pizza form, and I hope including recipes like this in this book inspires you to think about your favorites and do the same.

To keep the pizza from getting soggy, remove as much moisture from the fresh mozzarella as possible by breaking it into small pieces and laying them down onto a few layers of paper towels at least 1 hour before cooking. To help draw out even more moisture, lay another paper towel on top as well.

Cook the hot dog according to the instructions on the packaging. (If you are using a standard sausage, cook this in your home oven or in a frying pan until it is cooked through and just starting to brown on the outside.) Once cooked, allow your hot dog to cool before thinly slicing. Set aside.

Fire up your Ooni pizza oven, and aim for a stone temperature of 800 to 840°F (430 to 450°C). Depending on the outside temperature, this should take approximately 20 minutes. In the colder months, an extra 10 to 15 minutes might be needed. You can check the stone temperature with an infrared thermometer.

When the stone has reached approximately 750°F (400°C), stretch out the dough ball using the instructions on page 21.

Add the tomato sauce to the center of the base and spread in a circular motion, moving out toward the crust using the back of your spoon. Next, evenly add the Grana Padano and fresh mozzarella before a drizzle of oil. You can add your sliced hot dog at this point, but to avoid the possibility of it burning, I prefer to add it post-bake.

(continued)

HOT DIGGITY DOG PIZZA (CONTINUED)

Give your chosen pizza peel a light dusting of semolina flour before transferring the dough onto it. You can do this by lying the peel flat alongside the dough, and then, using both hands, gently lift the edge of the dough and slide it onto the peel. This stage can be daunting, but be confident and do it in one smooth, quick movement. After sliding the dough onto the peel, give it a final reshape. If you don't feel confident enough to use this technique, you can place the stretched-out dough straight onto the floured peel after stretching it over your knuckles and top while it is on the peel.

When the stone temperature has reached 800 to 840°F (430 to 450°C), give the peel a little shuffle/shake to ensure the dough isn't sticking, and then launch confidently into the middle of your Ooni pizza oven. Do not take your eyes off the pizza, as a few seconds can make a big difference to the overall bake!

After approximately 20 seconds, you will begin to see the crust at the back of the oven start to brown/blister. Warm the metal peel/turning peel in the back of the oven by holding it in the flames for a few seconds. (This will help stop the peel from sticking to the bottom of the pizza.) Then, carefully slide it under the pizza and turn it 180 degrees. When the crust that is now at the back of the oven starts to brown/blister, turn the pizza again, but this time, 90 degrees. Finally, do one last 180-degree turn so that all of the pizza has an even bake. The total cooking time should be 60 to 90 seconds.

Remove the pizza from the oven and slide it onto a cooling rack for 1 to 2 minutes before transferring to a display board. If you haven't added the sliced hot dog pre-bake, evenly add it before adding a drizzle of yellow mustard. (I like to do this in a nice and neat zigzag pattern.) Finish off with a sprinkle of crispy onions. Cut into 6 slices and serve hot.

WOULD YOU LIKE FRIES ON THAT PIZZA?

YIELD: 1 pizza (serves 1-2)

56 g (½ cup) fresh mozzarella

100 g (⅔ cup) fries

1 (275-g) ball Neapolitan Dough (page 19)

2–3 tbsp (30–45 ml) Keep-It-Simple Tomato Sauce (page 35)

1 tsp finely grated Grana Padano

Drizzle of extra virgin olive oil

Fine semolina flour

Sprinkle of sea salt

No, your eyes are not deceiving you. That is a pizza with fries on top of it! Many of you may be thinking that this is just not right, but stick with me and you may just come to love it! After all, if you like pizza and you like fries, what's not to love? How this recipe came about is a funny story. After a night out with my friends a few years ago, I called to get some food from a local takeout before I went home. I couldn't decide whether to have a pizza or fries (you probably know what's coming next), so the person serving me suggested I have the fries on the pizza, and wow, what a suggestion that was! While I thought I had invented a classic, a trip to Italy a year later taught me that fries on a pizza is very traditional in Italy and is known as *pizza wurstel e patatine* or *Americana*, which also has sliced sausages on it.

To keep the pizza from getting soggy, remove as much moisture from the fresh mozzarella as possible by breaking it into small pieces and laying them down onto a few layers of paper towels at least 1 hour before cooking. To help draw out even more moisture, lay another paper towel on top as well.

Fire up your Ooni pizza oven, and aim for a stone temperature of 800 to 840°F (430 to 450°C). Depending on the outside temperature, this should take approximately 20 minutes. In the colder months, an extra 10 to 15 minutes might be needed. You can check the stone temperature using an infrared thermometer.

While your Ooni pizza oven is heating up, cook your fries. You can use frozen fries cooked in your home oven or make your own using a fryer. Whichever you do, aim for the fries to have just finished cooking when your pizza comes out of the Ooni pizza oven. This is to make sure they are still hot when you add them to the pizza. If you want to add any seasoning or spice to the fries, do this as soon as they come out of the oven/fryer.

When the stone has reached approximately 750°F (400°C), stretch out the dough ball using the instructions on page 21.

Add the tomato sauce to the center of the base and spread in a circular motion, moving out toward the crust using the back of your spoon. Next, evenly add the Grana Padano and fresh mozzarella before a drizzle of oil. As the fries will be added to the pizza post-bake, this will be baked as a Margherita, so place slightly larger pieces of mozzarella in the center of the pizza. This is to help stop the base from doming during the bake.

(continued)

WOULD YOU LIKE FRIES ON THAT PIZZA? (CONTINUED)

Give your chosen pizza peel a light dusting of semolina flour before transferring the dough onto it. You can do this by lying the peel flat alongside the dough, and then, using both hands, gently lift the edge of the dough and slide it onto the peel. This stage can be daunting, but be confident and do it in one smooth, quick movement. After sliding the dough onto the peel, give it a final reshape. If you don't feel confident enough to use this technique, you can place the stretched-out dough straight onto the floured peel after stretching it over your knuckles and top while it is on the peel.

When the stone temperature has reached 800 to 840°F (430 to 450°C), give the peel a little shuffle/shake to ensure the dough isn't sticking, and then launch confidently into the middle of your Ooni pizza oven. Do not take your eyes off the pizza, as a few seconds can make a big difference to the overall bake!

After approximately 20 seconds, you will begin to see the crust at the back of the oven start to brown/blister. Warm the metal peel/turning peel in the back of the oven by holding it in the flames for a few seconds. (This will help stop the peel from sticking to the bottom of the pizza.) Then, carefully slide it under the pizza and turn it 180 degrees. When the crust that is now at the back of the oven starts to brown/blister, turn the pizza again, but this time, 90 degrees. Finally, do one last 180-degree turn so that all of the pizza has an even bake. The total cooking time should be 60 to 90 seconds. If at any point the base does start to dome up, don't worry. Just slide the metal peel/turning peel under the base to release the trapped air.

Remove the pizza from the oven and slide it onto a cooling rack for 1 to 2 minutes before transferring to a display board. Add the fries evenly around the pizza before finishing off with a sprinkle of sea salt (if not already seasoned/flavored). Cut into 6 slices and serve hot.

PUMPKIN, SPICE AND ALL THINGS NICE

YIELD: 1 pizza (serves 1-2)

For the Pumpkin Puree

1 small pumpkin

1 tbsp (15 ml) honey

1 tsp crushed red pepper flakes

30 ml (⅛ cup) heavy cream (double cream)

For the Pizza

56 g (½ cup) fresh mozzarella

1 (275-g) ball Neapolitan Dough (page 19)

Fresh basil leaves, soaked in salt water*

10 g blue cheese, chopped into small pieces

15 g 'nduja, broken into small pieces**

Drizzle of extra virgin olive oil

Fine semolina flour

1 tsp crushed red pepper flakes

* Soaking the basil leaves in salt water protects them from burning, since they are added before baking.

** See my Hot and Creamy 'Nduja recipe on page 51 for more information on this awesome sausage.

The next time you're out picking pumpkins, be sure to pick up an extra one for this recipe! Pumpkin puree on a pizza might sound strange, but once it's been spiked with honey and crushed red pepper flakes, it works perfectly as a base sauce. I have experimented with a few different toppings to pair with pumpkin, and I have found that big flavors work well. And they don't get much bigger than the almighty 'nduja! Remember that this pizza doesn't have to be confined to just once a year around Halloween. Pumpkin puree is readily available in grocery stores (typically in 400-g cans), and you can also swap out pumpkin for its cousin, butternut squash.

Preheat your home oven to of 400°F (200°C).

Cut the pumpkin in half with a sharp knife, and scoop out the seeds and as much of the stringy bits as possible. Place the pumpkin halves cut-side-down onto a baking tray lined with parchment paper, and cook for 45 to 60 minutes, or until the flesh can be easily pierced with a knife and the skin comes away from the flesh.

Scoop out the flesh into a food processor, and add the honey, red pepper flakes and cream. Blend until smooth, and store in an airtight container in the fridge for up to 3 days. Remove the puree from the fridge a few hours before using to allow it to come to room temperature.

To keep the pizza from getting soggy, remove as much moisture from the fresh mozzarella as possible by breaking it into small pieces and laying them down onto a few layers of paper towels at least 1 hour before cooking. To help draw out even more moisture, lay another paper towel on top as well.

Fire up your Ooni pizza oven, and aim for a stone temperature of 800 to 840°F (430 to 450°C). Depending on the outside temperature, this should take approximately 20 minutes. In the colder months, an extra 10 to 15 minutes might be needed. You can check the stone temperature with an infrared thermometer.

When the stone has reached approximately 750°F (400°C), stretch out the dough ball using the instructions on page 21.

Add 61 grams (¼ cup) of the pumpkin puree to the center of the base and spread in a circular motion, moving out toward the crust using the back of your spoon. Evenly add the basil, mozzarella, blue cheese and 'nduja before a drizzle of oil.

(continued)

PUMPKIN, SPICE AND ALL THINGS NICE (CONTINUED)

Give your chosen pizza peel a light dusting of semolina flour before transferring the dough onto it. You can do this by lying the peel flat alongside the dough, and then, using both hands, gently lift the edge of the dough and slide it onto the peel. This stage can be daunting, but be confident and do it in one, smooth, quick movement. After sliding the dough onto the peel, give it a final reshape. If you don't feel confident enough to use this technique, you can place the stretched-out dough straight onto the floured peel after stretching it over your knuckles and top while it is on the peel.

When the stone temperature has reached 800 to 840°F (430 to 450°C), give the peel a little shuffle/shake to ensure the dough isn't sticking, and then launch confidently into the middle of your Ooni pizza oven. Do not take your eyes off the pizza, as a few seconds can make a big difference to the overall bake!

After approximately 20 seconds, you will begin to see the crust at the back of the oven start to brown/blister. Warm the metal peel/turning peel in the back of the oven by holding it in the flames for a few seconds. (This will help stop the peel from sticking to the bottom of the pizza.) Then, carefully slide it under the pizza and turn it 180 degrees. When the crust that is now at the back of the oven starts to brown/blister, turn the pizza again, but this time, 90 degrees. Finally, do one last 180-degree turn so that all of the pizza has an even bake. The total cooking time should be 60 to 90 seconds.

Remove the pizza from the oven and slide it onto a cooling rack for 1 to 2 minutes before transferring to a display board. Sprinkle the red pepper flakes all over the pizza to finish. Cut into 6 slices and serve hot.

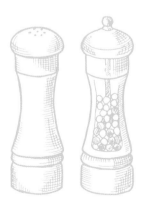

NOT JUST MUSHROOMS . . . BUT TRUFFLE MUSHROOMS

YIELD: 1 pizza (serves 1-2)

For the Truffle Mushrooms

2 tbsp (30 ml) truffle oil

14 g (1 tbsp) butter

1 clove garlic, crushed or finely chopped

23 g (⅓ cup) washed and thinly sliced mushrooms

Splash of lemon juice

1 tsp fresh thyme

For the Pizza

74 g (⅔ cup) fresh mozzarella

1 (275-g) ball Neapolitan Dough (page 19)

Fine semolina flour

1 tsp fresh thyme

Lemon zest, for garnishing

When it comes to using mushrooms as a pizza topping, there are two key things to remember: Always use fresh mushrooms, and don't use them raw. (The heat of the oven will cause them to dry out.) Sautéing mushrooms is a great way to pack in appetizing flavors while ensuring they stay nice and juicy. In this recipe, I use truffle oil, lemon juice, fresh thyme and garlic. (You can't have sautéed mushrooms without garlic, right?) If you don't have truffle oil, extra virgin olive oil will work, but the truffle oil takes this pizza from great to heavenly!

To keep the pizza from getting soggy, remove as much moisture from the fresh mozzarella as possible by breaking it into small pieces and laying them down onto a few layers of paper towels at least 1 hour before cooking. To help draw out even more moisture, lay another paper towel on top as well.

Fire up your Ooni pizza oven, and aim for a stone temperature of 800 to 840°F (430 to 450°C). Depending on the outside temperature, this should take approximately 20 minutes. In the colder months, an extra 10 to 15 minutes might be needed. You can check the stone temperature with an infrared thermometer.

While your Ooni pizza oven is heating up, make the mushrooms. Heat the truffle oil and butter in a skillet/frying pan over medium heat. Add the garlic and mushrooms and cook for 1 to 2 minutes until they are starting to soften. Turn the heat down to low and add a splash of lemon juice and the thyme, and toss so all the mushrooms are coated. Cook for 1 minute before taking the skillet/frying pan off the heat. Put the mushrooms and the remaining oil from the frying pan into a container and leave to one side to cool.

When the stone has reached approximately 750°F (400°C), stretch out the dough ball using the instructions on page 21.

Add the pieces of fresh mozzarella to the base making sure not to leave any big gaps. Since this pizza does not have a sauce to protect the base, it's important not to leave big areas of the base exposed. Evenly add the mushrooms before drizzling the remaining truffle oil you saved from the skillet/frying pan on top.

(continued)

NOT JUST MUSHROOMS ... BUT TRUFFLE MUSHROOMS (CONTINUED)

Give your chosen pizza peel a light dusting of semolina flour before transferring the dough onto it. You can do this by lying the peel flat alongside the dough, and then, using both hands, gently lift the edge of the dough and slide it onto the peel. This stage can be daunting, but be confident and do it in one smooth, quick movement. After sliding the dough onto the peel, give it a final reshape. If you don't feel confident enough to use this technique, you can place the stretched-out dough straight onto the floured peel after stretching it over your knuckles and top while it is on the peel.

When the stone temperature has reached 800 to 840°F (430 to 450°C), give the peel a little shuffle/shake to ensure the dough isn't sticking, and then launch confidently into the middle of your Ooni pizza oven. Do not take your eyes off the pizza, as a few seconds can make a big difference to the overall bake!

After approximately 20 seconds, you will begin to see the crust at the back of the oven start to brown/blister. Warm the metal peel/turning peel in the back of the oven by holding it in the flames for a few seconds. (This will help stop the peel from sticking to the bottom of the pizza.) Then, carefully slide it under the pizza and turn it 180 degrees. When the crust that is now at the back of the oven starts to brown/blister, turn the pizza again, but this time, 90 degrees. Finally, do one last 180-degree turn so that all of the pizza has an even bake. The total cooking time should be 60 to 90 seconds.

Remove the pizza from the oven and slide it onto a cooling rack for 1 to 2 minutes before transferring to a display board. Add the fresh thyme and grate some fresh lemon zest all over the pizza to finish. Cut into 6 slices and serve hot.

THE ALTERNATIVE HAWAIIAN

YIELD: 1 pizza (serves 1-2)

56 g (½ cup) fresh mozzarella
54 g (⅓ cup) sliced fresh pineapple
1 (275-g) ball Neapolitan Dough (page 19)
2-3 tbsp (30-45 ml) Keep-It-Simple Tomato Sauce (page 35)
1 tsp finely grated Grana Padano
30 g sliced pepperoni
Drizzle of extra virgin olive oil
Fine semolina flour

Does pineapple belong on pizza? This is an age-old question that completely divides us around the world and will probably rumble on until the end of time. My answer to that question is YES! It takes me back to family summer holidays where we would all take a break from the sun to eat beautiful slices of fresh pineapple from a local beach fruit seller. I understand that the thought of adding wet pineapple chunks to a pizza may not be appealing, but if you're willing to follow the steps in this recipe, you'll be joining Team Pineapple before you know it! I've switched out the more commonly used ham for pepperoni as I find the bit of spice from the pepperoni works wonders with the sweetness of the pineapple.

To keep the pizza from getting soggy, remove as much moisture from the fresh mozzarella as possible by breaking it into small pieces and laying them down onto a few layers of paper towels at least 1 hour before cooking. To help draw out even more moisture, lay another paper towel on top as well.

Fire up your Ooni pizza oven, and aim for a stone temperature of 800 to 840°F (430 to 450°C). Depending on the outside temperature, this should take approximately 20 minutes. In the colder months, an extra 10 to 15 minutes might be needed. You can check the stone temperature with an infrared thermometer.

When the stone temperature of the oven reaches 660°F (350°C), place a cast-iron skillet into the oven and heat it for 5 minutes. You want the skillet to be superhot! Remove the skillet and place on a heatproof surface. Put the slices of pineapple onto the skillet and cook for 1 to 2 minutes on each side. (You do not need to put the skillet back into the oven.) Once nicely charred, remove them from the skillet and cut into small pieces ready for topping.

When the stone has reached approximately 750°F (400°C), stretch out the dough ball using the instructions on page 21.

Add the tomato sauce to the center of the base and spread in a circular motion, moving out toward the crust using the back of your spoon. Next, evenly add the Grana Padano, fresh mozzarella, charred pineapple pieces and pepperoni before a drizzle of oil.

(continued)

THE ALTERNATIVE HAWAIIAN (CONTINUED)

Give your chosen pizza peel a light dusting of semolina flour before transferring the dough onto it. You can do this by lying the peel flat alongside the dough, and then, using both hands, gently lift the edge of the dough and slide it onto the peel. This stage can be daunting, but be confident and do it in one smooth, quick movement. After sliding the dough onto the peel, give it a final reshape. If you don't feel confident enough to use this technique, you can place the stretched-out dough straight onto the floured peel after stretching it over your knuckles and top while it is on the peel.

When the stone temperature has reached 800 to 840°F (430 to 450°C), give the peel a little shuffle/shake to ensure the dough isn't sticking, and then launch confidently into the middle of your Ooni pizza oven. Do not take your eyes off the pizza, as a few seconds can make a big difference to the overall bake!

After approximately 20 seconds, you will begin to see the crust at the back of the oven start to brown/blister. Warm the metal peel/turning peel in the back of the oven by holding it in the flames for a few seconds. (This will help stop the peel from sticking to the bottom of the pizza.) Then, carefully slide it under the pizza and turn it 180 degrees. When the crust that is now at the back of the oven starts to brown/blister, turn the pizza again, but this time, 90 degrees. Finally, do one last 180-degree turn so that all of the pizza has an even bake. The total cooking time should be 60 to 90 seconds.

Remove the pizza from the oven and slide it onto a cooling rack for 1 to 2 minutes before transferring to a display board. Cut into 6 slices and serve hot.

A TASTE OF MOROCCO

YIELD: 1 pizza (serves 1-2)

For the Moroccan Lamb

1 tbsp (15 ml) extra virgin olive oil

1 clove garlic, crushed or finely chopped

40 g (¼ cup) finely chopped onion

200 g minced ground lamb

Salt and pepper, as desired

2 g (2 tsp) paprika

½ tsp ground cinnamon

1 tbsp (9 g) finely chopped dried apricots

6 tbsp (90 ml) Keep-It-Simple Tomato Sauce (page 35)

For the Pizza

1 (275-g) ball Neapolitan Dough (page 19)

Drizzle of extra virgin olive oil

Fine semolina flour

10 g (1 tbsp) feta cheese

Handful of chopped fresh mint

I know minced lamb is not your average pizza topping, but one bite of this pizza will have your taste buds singing and wanting more. While I haven't visited Morocco, I am a huge fan of the flavors used in Moroccan cuisine. My favorite dish is the iconic tagine, which is a slow cooked, succulent stew/hot pot (usually made with lamb), that is absolutely packed full of intense flavors and spices. As a tagine can take many hours to cook, for this recipe, I have taken all the amazing flavors and created my own quick-and-easy version as a pizza topping. I challenge anyone to glance over the ingredient list on the left and not be immediately filled with excitement and anticipation at the thought of that first bite!

Fire up your Ooni pizza oven, and aim for a stone temperature of 800 to 840°F (430 to 450°C). Depending on the outside temperature, this should take approximately 20 minutes. In the colder months, an extra 10 to 15 minutes might be needed. You can check the stone temperature with an infrared thermometer.

While your Ooni pizza oven is heating up, in a skillet/frying pan, heat the oil over a medium heat. Add the garlic, onion, lamb, salt and pepper, and fry until it starts to brown. Drain off the excess fat, then stir in the paprika, cinnamon, chopped apricots and tomato sauce. Cook for 2 minutes. Remove the lamb from the skillet/frying pan, and let it cool.

When the stone has reached approximately 750°F (400°C), stretch out the dough ball using the instructions on page 21.

Add the lamb to the base and spread it out toward the crust using the back of your spoon. Add a drizzle of oil.

Give your chosen pizza peel a light dusting of semolina flour before transferring the dough onto it. You can do this by lying the peel flat alongside the dough, and then, using both hands, gently lift the edge of the dough and slide it onto the peel. This stage can be daunting, but be confident and do it in one smooth, quick movement. After sliding the dough onto the peel, give it a final reshape. If you don't feel confident enough to use this technique, you can place the stretched-out dough straight onto the floured peel after stretching it over your knuckles and top while it is on the peel.

(continued)

A TASTE OF MOROCCO
(CONTINUED)

When the stone temperature has reached 800 to 840°F (430 to 450°C), give the peel a little shuffle/shake to ensure the dough isn't sticking, and then launch confidently into the middle of your Ooni pizza oven. Do not take your eyes off the pizza, as a few seconds can make a big difference to the overall bake!

After approximately 20 seconds, you will begin to see the crust at the back of the oven start to brown/blister. Warm the metal peel/turning peel in the back of the oven by holding it in the flames for a few seconds. (This will help stop the peel from sticking to the bottom of the pizza.) Then, carefully slide it under the pizza and turn it 180 degrees. When the crust that is now at the back of the oven starts to brown/blister, turn the pizza again, but this time, 90 degrees. Finally, do one last 180-degree turn so that all of the pizza has an even bake. The total cooking time should be 60 to 90 seconds.

Remove the pizza from the oven and slide it onto a cooling rack for 1 to 2 minutes before transferring to a display board. Crumble the feta cheese evenly over the pizza before finishing off with a sprinkle of freshy chopped mint leaves. Cut into 6 slices and serve hot.

NEW YORK, NEW YORK

When I think of a New York style pizza, I instantly think of the movie *Home Alone 2: Lost in New York*, where Kevin McCallister is served his "very own cheese pizza" for his limousine ride exploring Manhattan. That iconic moment when the pizza box is opened to reveal his steaming hot pizza will live long in my memory, and I'm sure it's one of the main reasons a plain cheese pizza is one of my all-time favorites.

Walking the bustling streets of New York, you will see an abundance of people with plain cheese or pepperoni pizza served by the slice on a paper plate and then folded in half so it can be eaten on the go. Although New York pizza is derived from the Italian Neapolitan style, it has several different characteristics—most notably the smaller, chewier crust and how when held, the slice doesn't flop like a Neapolitan slice does. While I am fortunate enough to have been to, and eaten pizza in, New York, it was unfortunately a long time ago, way before my pizza journey started and became such a big part of my life. I am very keen to go back so I can visit and experience pizza from some of the most famous pizzerias in the world.

While Ooni pizza ovens are most known for making Neapolitan style pizzas, their ability to cook at lower temperatures also makes them ideal for cooking New York style pizzas.In this chapter, you will find some iconic New York pizza topping combinations, but also some that are a little different, from the renowned tomato and barbecue-based pizzas (Barbecue Chicken on page 107), to one where I actually flip the toppings upside-down (Upside-Down Margherita on page 101)! Fear not though, all these recipes will have your taste buds tingling, including one of my favorite pizzas, the Chorizo, Fennel Sausage and Ricotta (page 105), where I use some beautiful lemon-infused ricotta.

A PLAIN CHEESE PIZZA JUST FOR ME

YIELD: 1 pizza (serves 1-2)

2-3 tbsp (30-45 ml) Keep-It-Simple Tomato Sauce (page 35)

½ tsp garlic powder

1 tsp dried oregano, plus extra for garnishing

16 g (1 tbsp) tomato puree

1 (260-g) ball New York Dough (page 22)

112 g (1 cup) freshly grated low-moisture mozzarella

Fine semolina flour

A large slice of a New York-style plain cheese pizza is very hard to beat, and when made properly, it will always be the ultimate crowd-pleaser. Don't be fooled by the word "plain" in the recipe title . . . this pizza is anything but plain. The chewy crust, sweet tomatoes and creamy cheese are a match made in pizza heaven. Ever since watching Kevin McCallister with his "very own" cheese pizza in the *Home Alone* movies as a young child, this has always been my go-to pizza. In fact, I loved this pizza so much growing up that I don't think I added toppings until I reached adulthood (other than the occasional pepperoni pizza)!

A good tip is to keep the cheese in the fridge until it is required. Using the cheese cold will help prevent it from burning too much in your Ooni pizza oven. I also recommend using a block of mozzarella and grating it yourself rather than using a pre-grated variety. The packets of pre-grated mozzarella are often coated with a powder to prevent it from sticking in the bag, which will cause it to burn much quicker.

Fire up your Ooni pizza oven, and aim for a stone temperature of 750 to 790°F (400 to 420°C). Depending on the outside temperature, this should take approximately 15 to 20 minutes. In the colder months, an extra 10 to 15 minutes might be needed. You can check the stone temperature with an infrared thermometer.

While your Ooni pizza oven is heating up, make the sauce. In a bowl, combine the sauce, garlic powder, oregano and tomato puree and stir until combined.

When the stone has reached approximately 720°F (380°C), stretch out the dough ball using the instructions on page 25.

Add the sauce to the center of the base and spread in a circular motion, moving out toward the crust using the back of your spoon. Remove the grated mozzarella from the fridge, and evenly add it to the base, making sure you go right up to where the crust begins.

Give your chosen pizza peel a light dusting of semolina flour before transferring the dough onto it. You can do this by lying the peel flat alongside the dough, and then, using both hands, gently lift the edge of the dough and slide it onto the peel. This stage can be daunting, but be confident and do it in one smooth, quick movement. After sliding the dough onto the peel, give it a final reshape. If you don't feel confident enough to use this technique, you can place the stretched-out dough straight onto the floured peel after stretching it over your knuckles and top while it is on the peel.

(continued)

A PLAIN CHEESE PIZZA JUST FOR ME (CONTINUED)

If you are using a gas-powered oven, when the stone temperature has reached 750 to 790°F (400 to 420°C), give the peel a little shuffle/shake to ensure the dough isn't sticking, and then launch confidently into the middle of your Ooni pizza oven. Immediately turn the flame off, and cook in the residual heat for 2 minutes, turning 180 degrees halfway through. After 2 minutes, turn the flame back on to low, and cook for 4 to 5 minutes, turning 90 degrees every 45 to 60 seconds. If the crust needs a little bit more color, turn the flame up to high, and cook for 30 to 60 seconds, turning regularly to achieve a nice, even bake.

If you are using a wood/charcoal or pellet powered oven, aim to get the stone temperature to around 840°F (450°C), and then stop adding fuel so that the flames begin to die down. Once the flames are low (or have even died down completely) and the stone temperature has reduced to 750 to 790°F (400 to 420°C), give the peel a little shuffle/shake to ensure the dough isn't sticking. Launch your pizza confidently into the middle of your Ooni pizza oven and cook for 3 to 4 minutes, turning 90 degrees after approximately every minute. A good indication that the pizza is ready for the first turn is when the bottom of the pizza starts to form a rounded lip where it is in contact with the stone. To finish off the pizza, add a chunk of wood (or additional pellets) to the oven to spike the flames and cook for 1 to 2 minutes, turning regularly to achieve a nice, even bake. To make sure this chunk of wood ignites instantly, place it inside your oven directly on the stone (to one side so it isn't in the way) for 1 minute, so it warms up before using your peel to place it into the fuel tray from inside your oven.

Remove the pizza from the oven and slide it onto a cooling rack for 1 to 2 minutes before transferring to a display board. Sprinkle dried oregano to finish. Cut into 6 slices and serve hot.

UPSIDE-DOWN MARGHERITA

YIELD: 1 pizza (serves 1-2)

2-3 tbsp (30-45 ml) Keep-It-Simple Tomato Sauce (page 35)

1 tsp garlic powder

1 tsp dried oregano

16 g (1 tbsp) tomato puree

1 (260-g) ball New York Dough (page 22)

112 g (1 cup) sliced low-moisture mozzarella

Fine semolina flour

Drizzle of garlic oil

Fresh basil leaves

1 tsp finely grated Grana Padano

It may seem strange that I've included a separate recipe for a pizza using nearly the exact same toppings as A Plain Cheese Pizza Just for Me (page 99), but simply flipping the toppings upside-down creates a whole new taste and eating experience. Initially your taste buds will be confused, as you will be subconsciously expecting to taste creamy cheese first, but what comes is a sweet flavor from the tomato sauce. After the confusion subsides, your taste buds will be thanking you and craving more. To ensure I always achieve a nice, even bake, I never take my eyes off the pizza once it is launched it into my oven. By doing this, you will get to see all the different stages of the pizza cooking. I love the point in this bake where the cheese begins to bubble and break through the layer of tomato sauce.

Fire up your Ooni pizza oven, and aim for a stone temperature of 750 to 790°F (400 to 420°C). Depending on the outside temperature, this should take approximately 15 to 20 minutes. In the colder months, an extra 10 to 15 minutes might be needed. You can check the stone temperature with an infrared thermometer.

While your Ooni pizza oven is heating up, make the sauce. In a bowl, combine the sauce, garlic powder, oregano and tomato puree and stir until combined.

When the stone has reached approximately 720°F (380°C), stretch out the dough ball using the instructions on page 25.

Add the slices of low moisture mozzarella to the base. Add dollops of the tomato sauce on top of the mozzarella and in any gaps. Use the back of your spoon to spread the sauce around. You won't hear me say this very often as I love when everything looks neat and symmetrical, but don't worry about spreading the sauce evenly here as I personally think having it a bit uneven adds to the finished look of this pizza.

Give your chosen pizza peel a light dusting of semolina flour before transferring the dough onto it. You can do this by lying the peel flat alongside the dough, and then, using both hands, gently lift the edge of the dough and slide it onto the peel. This stage can be daunting, but be confident and do it in one smooth, quick movement. After sliding the dough onto the peel, give it a final reshape. If you don't feel confident enough to use this technique, you can place the stretched-out dough straight onto the floured peel after stretching it over your knuckles and top while it is on the peel.

(continued)

UPSIDE-DOWN MARGHERITA (CONTINUED)

If you are using a gas-powered oven, when the stone temperature has reached 750 to 790°F (400 to 420°C), give the peel a little shuffle/shake to ensure the dough isn't sticking, and then launch confidently into the middle of your Ooni pizza oven. Immediately turn the flame off, and cook in the residual heat for 2 minutes, turning 180 degrees halfway through. After 2 minutes, turn the flame back on to low, and cook for 4 to 5 minutes, turning 90 degrees every 45 to 60 seconds. If the crust needs a little bit more color, turn the flame up to high, and cook for 30 to 60 seconds, turning regularly to achieve a nice, even bake.

If you are using a wood/charcoal or pellet powered oven, aim to get the stone temperature to around 840°F (450°C), and then stop adding fuel so that the flames begin to die down. Once the flames are low (or have even died down completely) and the stone temperature has reduced to 750 to 790°F (400 to 420°C), give the peel a little shuffle/shake to ensure the dough isn't sticking. Launch your pizza confidently into the middle of your Ooni pizza oven and cook for 3 to 4 minutes, turning 90 degrees after approximately every minute. A good indication that the pizza is ready for the first turn is when the bottom of the pizza starts to form a rounded lip where it is in contact with the stone. To finish off the pizza, add a chunk of wood (or additional pellets) to the oven to spike the flames and cook for 1 to 2 minutes, turning regularly to achieve a nice, even bake. To make sure this chunk of wood ignites instantly, place it inside your oven directly on the stone (to one side so it isn't in the way) for 1 minute, so it warms up before using your peel to place it into the fuel tray from inside your oven.

Remove the pizza from the oven and slide it onto a cooling rack for 1 to 2 minutes before transferring to a display board. Add a drizzle of garlic oil, fresh basil leaves and a generous grating of Grana Padano to finish. Cut into 6 slices and serve hot.

CHORIZO, FENNEL SAUSAGE AND RICOTTA

YIELD: 1 pizza (serves 1-2)

¼ tsp fennel seeds

1-2 sausages

1 tsp vegetable oil

185 g (¾ cup) ricotta

½ tsp lemon juice

Pinch of salt

2-3 tbsp (30-45 ml) Keep-It-Simple Tomato Sauce (page 35)

½ tsp garlic powder

1 tsp dried oregano

16 g (1 tbsp) tomato puree

1 (260-g) ball New York Dough (page 22)

74 g (⅔ cup) freshly grated low-moisture mozzarella

30 g chorizo, cut into small cubes

Drizzle of extra virgin olive oil

Fine semolina flour

Drizzle of hot honey

Sometimes multiple bold flavors and textures can compete, resulting in an unpleasant eating experience. Not here though! All the flavors and textures in this recipe work in perfect harmony. The lemon-infused ricotta added post-bake finishes off this pizza to perfection. I experimented with a few different types of cured meats before finally settling on chorizo. This recipe was inspired by Tony Gemignani's New Yorker pizza. I have admired Tony since I first started my pizza journey.

You may have noticed that many of the pizzas in this book remind me of fond childhood memories. Well, when I'm grinding the fennel seeds for the sausage, the aroma takes me back to not being able to resist my mums' bag of aniseed sweets she was always stocked up on. Sorry, mum!

With a pestle and mortar, grind the fennel seeds to form a coarse powder. If you don't have a pestle and mortar, place the fennel seeds onto a chopping board, cover with a kitchen towel and carefully bash using a rolling pin. Remove the sausage(s) from their skins and place into a bowl. Add the fennel to the sausage, and mix with a fork until combined.

Heat the vegetable oil in a skillet/frying pan over medium heat. With wet fingers, break the sausage meat into small pieces, and add them to the skillet/frying pan. Cook for 2 to 4 minutes, or until they start to brown. Remove the sausage from the skillet/frying pan and allow to cool.

Place the ricotta, lemon juice and salt into a small container and mix together. Once combined, spoon the ricotta into a piping bag with a round nozzle inside, and set aside. If you haven't got a round nozzle, you can just cut a hole in the end of the piping bag.

Fire up your Ooni pizza oven, and aim for a stone temperature of 750 to 790°F (400 to 420°C). Depending on the outside temperature, this should take approximately 15 to 20 minutes. In the colder months, an extra 10 to 15 minutes might be needed. You can check the stone temperature with an infrared thermometer.

While your Ooni pizza oven is heating up, make the sauce. In a bowl, combine the sauce, garlic powder, oregano and tomato puree and stir until combined.

When the stone has reached approximately 720°F (380°C), stretch out the dough ball using the instructions on page 25.

Add the tomato sauce to the center of the base and spread in a circular motion, moving out toward the crust using the back of your spoon. Next, evenly add the mozzarella, fennel sausage and chorizo before a drizzle of oil.

(continued)

CHORIZO, FENNEL SAUSAGE AND RICOTTA (CONTINUED)

Give your chosen pizza peel a light dusting of semolina flour before transferring the dough onto it. You can do this by lying the peel flat alongside the dough, and then, using both hands, gently lift the edge of the dough and slide it onto the peel. This stage can be daunting, but be confident and do it in one smooth, quick movement. After sliding the dough onto the peel, give it a final reshape. If you don't feel confident enough to use this technique, you can place the stretched-out dough straight onto the floured peel after stretching it over your knuckles and top while it is on the peel.

If you are using a gas-powered oven, when the stone temperature has reached 750 to 790°F (400 to 420°C), give the peel a little shuffle/shake to ensure the dough isn't sticking, and then launch confidently into the middle of your Ooni pizza oven. Immediately turn the flame off, and cook in the residual heat for 2 minutes, turning 180 degrees halfway through. After 2 minutes, turn the flame back on to low, and cook for 4 to 5 minutes, turning 90 degrees every 45 to 60 seconds. If the crust needs a little bit more color, turn the flame up to high, and cook for 30 to 60 seconds, turning regularly to achieve a nice, even bake.

If you are using a wood/charcoal or pellet powered oven, aim to get the stone temperature to around 840°F (450°C), and then stop adding fuel so that the flames begin to die down. Once the flames are low (or have even died down completely) and the stone temperature has reduced to 750 to 790°F (400 to 420°C), give the peel a little shuffle/shake to ensure the dough isn't sticking. Launch your pizza confidently into the middle of your Ooni pizza oven and cook for 3 to 4 minutes, turning 90 degrees after approximately every minute. A good indication that the pizza is ready for the first turn is when the bottom of the pizza starts to form a rounded lip where it is in contact with the stone. To finish off the pizza, add a chunk of wood (or additional pellets) to the oven to spike the flames and cook for 1 to 2 minutes, turning regularly to achieve a nice, even bake. To make sure this chunk of wood ignites instantly, place it inside your oven directly on the stone (to one side so it isn't in the way) for 1 minute, so it warms up before using your peel to place it into the fuel tray from inside your oven.

Remove the pizza from the oven and slide it onto a cooling rack for 1 to 2 minutes before transferring to a display board. Cut into 6 slices and, using your piping bag, add three dollops of the lemon-infused ricotta onto each slice before finishing with a generous drizzle of hot honey.

BARBECUE CHICKEN

YIELD: 1 pizza (serves 1-2)

1 (260-g) ball New York Dough (page 22)

2–3 tbsp (30–45 ml) barbecue sauce

74 g (⅔ cup) freshly grated low-moisture mozzarella

80 g roast chicken, cut into small pieces

1 small red onion, sliced into circles

Fine semolina flour

Handful of chopped coriander or cilantro

This recipe was inspired by MANY visits to a popular New York–style restaurant close to where I live. I would order their barbecue chicken pizza (with a side of fries) every time without fail! Whenever I am making a batch of New York–style pizzas for friends and family, I always like to make sure there is at least one barbecue option, as I think it's nice to have a variety of flavors. I love how the red onion and chopped coriander give this pizza a vibrant color, but they also add a nice touch of freshness. If you're not a fan of coriander (or cilantro), a good alternative is finely chopped chives.

Fire up your Ooni pizza oven, and aim for a stone temperature of 750 to 790°F (400 to 420°C). Depending on the outside temperature, this should take approximately 15 to 20 minutes. In the colder months, an extra 10 to 15 minutes might be needed. You can check the stone temperature with an infrared thermometer.

When the stone has reached approximately 720°F (380°C), stretch out the dough ball using the instructions on page 25.

Add the barbecue sauce to the center of the base and spread in a circular motion, moving out toward the crust using the back of your spoon. Evenly add the mozzarella, making sure you go right up to where the crust begins, followed by the chicken and sliced red onion.

Give your chosen pizza peel a light dusting of semolina flour before transferring the dough onto it. You can do this by lying the peel flat alongside the dough, and then, using both hands, gently lift the edge of the dough and slide it onto the peel. This stage can be daunting, but be confident and do it in one smooth, quick movement. After sliding the dough onto the peel, give it a final reshape. If you don't feel confident enough to use this technique, you can place the stretched-out dough straight onto the floured peel after stretching it over your knuckles and top while it is on the peel.

If you are using a gas-powered oven, when the stone temperature has reached 750 to 790°F (400 to 420°C), give the peel a little shuffle/shake to ensure the dough isn't sticking, and then launch confidently into the middle of your Ooni pizza oven. Immediately turn the flame off, and cook in the residual heat for 2 minutes, turning 180 degrees halfway through. After 2 minutes, turn the flame back on to low, and cook for 4 to 5 minutes, turning 90 degrees every 45 to 60 seconds. If the crust needs a little bit more color, turn the flame up to high, and cook for 30 to 60 seconds, turning regularly to achieve a nice, even bake.

(continued)

BARBECUE CHICKEN (CONTINUED)

If you are using a wood/charcoal or pellet powered oven, aim to get the stone temperature to around 840°F (450°C), and then stop adding fuel so that the flames begin to die down. Once the flames are low (or have even died down completely) and the stone temperature has reduced to 750 to 790°F (400 to 420°C), give the peel a little shuffle/shake to ensure the dough isn't sticking. Launch your pizza confidently into the middle of your Ooni pizza oven and cook for 3 to 4 minutes, turning 90 degrees after approximately every minute. A good indication that the pizza is ready for the first turn is when the bottom of the pizza starts to form a rounded lip where it is in contact with the stone. To finish off the pizza, add a chunk of wood (or additional pellets) to the oven to spike the flames and cook for 1 to 2 minutes, turning regularly to achieve a nice, even bake. To make sure this chunk of wood ignites instantly, place it inside your oven directly on the stone (to one side so it isn't in the way) for 1 minute, so it warms up before using your peel to place it into the fuel tray from inside your oven.

Remove the pizza from the oven and slide it onto a cooling rack for 1 to 2 minutes before transferring to a display board. Finish by adding the chopped coriander. Cut into 6 slices and serve hot.

MIXED TOMATO BIANCA

YIELD: 1 pizza (serves 1-2)

1 (260-g) ball New York Dough (page 22)

112 g (1 cup) freshly grated low-moisture mozzarella

1 clove garlic, finely sliced

75 g (½ cup) chopped tomatoes*

Drizzle of extra virgin olive oil

Fine semolina flour

Handful of chopped basil

Pinch of sea salt

* If you are using small tomatoes, chop them in half. If the tomatoes you are using are larger, thinly slice them to prevent them from adding too much weight and moisture to the pizza.

With this pizza using just cheese, tomatoes and basil, you could classify it as a Margherita. While I absolutely love a Margherita (I'm sure you do too), this is totally different, with its very own unique flavor profile. This used to be a pizza I made as a Neapolitan style, but I have since developed it into this New York style recipe. I think the tomatoes really benefit from the extra time in the oven as they become softer with a more intense flavor. While you can use any tomatoes you like, I like to visit my local fruit and vegetable stand to see what different colors and varieties of tomatoes they have in order to make this as colorful as I can.

Fire up your Ooni pizza oven, and aim for a stone temperature of 750 to 790°F (400 to 420°C). Depending on the outside temperature, this should take approximately 15 to 20 minutes. In the colder months, an extra 10 to 15 minutes might be needed. You can check the stone temperature with an infrared thermometer.

When the stone has reached approximately 720°F (380°C), stretch out the dough ball using the instructions on page 25.

Add the grated mozzarella, making sure you go right up to where the crust begins. Evenly add the garlic and tomatoes before a drizzle of oil.

Give your chosen pizza peel a light dusting of semolina flour before transferring the dough onto it. You can do this by lying the peel flat alongside the dough, and then, using both hands, gently lift the edge of the dough and slide it onto the peel. This stage can be daunting, but be confident and do it in one smooth, quick movement. After sliding the dough onto the peel, give it a final reshape. If you don't feel confident enough to use this technique, you can place the stretched-out dough straight onto the floured peel after stretching it over your knuckles and top while it is on the peel.

If you are using a gas-powered oven, when the stone temperature has reached 750 to 790°F (400 to 420°C), give the peel a little shuffle/shake to ensure the dough isn't sticking, and then launch confidently into the middle of your Ooni pizza oven. Immediately turn the flame off, and cook in the residual heat for 2 minutes, turning 180 degrees halfway through. After 2 minutes, turn the flame back on to low, and cook for 4 to 5 minutes, turning 90 degrees every 45 to 60 seconds. If the crust needs a little bit more color, turn the flame up to high, and cook for 30 to 60 seconds, turning regularly to achieve a nice, even bake.

(continued)

MIXED TOMATO BIANCA
(CONTINUED)

If you are using a wood/charcoal or pellet powered oven, aim to get the stone temperature to around 840°F (450°C), and then stop adding fuel so that the flames begin to die down. Once the flames are low (or have even died down completely) and the stone temperature has reduced to 750 to 790°F (400 to 420°C), give the peel a little shuffle/shake to ensure the dough isn't sticking. Launch your pizza confidently into the middle of your Ooni pizza oven and cook for 3 to 4 minutes, turning 90 degrees after approximately every minute. A good indication that the pizza is ready for the first turn is when the bottom of the pizza starts to form a rounded lip where it is in contact with the stone. To finish off the pizza, add a chunk of wood (or additional pellets) to the oven to spike the flames and cook for 1 to 2 minutes, turning regularly to achieve a nice, even bake. To make sure this chunk of wood ignites instantly, place it inside your oven directly on the stone (to one side so it isn't in the way) for 1 minute, so it warms up before using your peel to place it into the fuel tray from inside your oven.

Remove the pizza from the oven and slide it onto a cooling rack for 1 to 2 minutes before transferring to a display board. Add the chopped basil and a pinch of sea salt to finish. Cut into 6 slices and serve hot.

SWEET AND SPICY 'RONI

YIELD: 1 pizza (serves 1-2)

2-3 tbsp (30-45 ml) Keep-It-Simple Tomato Sauce (page 35)

½ tsp garlic powder

1 tsp dried oregano, plus extra for garnishing

16 g (1 tbsp) tomato puree

1 (260-g) ball New York Dough (page 22)

74 g (⅔ cup) grated low moisture mozzarella

40 g sliced pepperoni

Fine semolina flour

Drizzle of hot honey

I couldn't do a whole chapter dedicated to New Yok style pizza recipes without having the classic pepperoni. Pepperoni is one of my favorite pizza toppings and arguably one of the world's most popular toppings, and for good reason. Growing up, I would very rarely deviate from a deliciously simple plain cheese pizza, but when I did, it would always be for pepperoni. This would normally be after watching an episode of one of my favorite TV shows: *Teenage Mutant Ninja Turtles*. They were famous for eating pizzas topped with all sorts of crazy combinations, but it was always the classic pepperoni that jumped out at me. When I'm using pepperoni, I don't like to add too many other flavors, apart from a touch of dried oregano, but one thing I have found that pairs incredibly well with it is hot honey. This touch of heat and sweetness leads to a very satisfying eating experience you will want to go back to time and time again!

Fire up your Ooni pizza oven, and aim for a stone temperature of 750 to 790°F (400 to 420°C). Depending on the outside temperature, this should take approximately 15 to 20 minutes. In the colder months, an extra 10 to 15 minutes might be needed. You can check the stone temperature with an infrared thermometer.

While your Ooni pizza oven is heating up, make the sauce. In a bowl, combine the sauce, garlic powder, oregano and tomato puree and stir until combined.

When the stone has reached approximately 720°F (380°C), stretch out the dough ball using the instructions on page 25.

Add the tomato sauce to the center of the base and spread in a circular motion, moving out toward the crust using the back of your spoon. Evenly add the mozzarella, making sure you go right up to where the crust begins, followed by the pepperoni. I like to go all out with the pepperoni and use enough so that you can't see any of the mozzarella or sauce underneath, but you can use as much or as little as you like.

Give your chosen pizza peel a light dusting of semolina flour before transferring the dough onto it. You can do this by lying the peel flat alongside the dough, and then, using both hands, gently lift the edge of the dough and slide it onto the peel. This stage can be daunting, but be confident and do it in one smooth, quick movement. After sliding the dough onto the peel, give it a final reshape. If you don't feel confident enough to use this technique, you can place the stretched-out dough straight onto the floured peel after stretching it over your knuckles and top while it is on the peel.

(continued)

SWEET AND SPICY 'RONI (CONTINUED)

If you are using a gas-powered oven, when the stone temperature has reached 750 to 790°F (400 to 420°C), give the peel a little shuffle/shake to ensure the dough isn't sticking, and then launch confidently into the middle of your Ooni pizza oven. Immediately turn the flame off, and cook in the residual heat for 2 minutes, turning 180 degrees halfway through. After 2 minutes, turn the flame back on to low, and cook for 4 to 5 minutes, turning 90 degrees every 45 to 60 seconds. If the crust needs a little bit more color, turn the flame up to high, and cook for 30 to 60 seconds, turning regularly to achieve a nice, even bake.

If you are using a wood/charcoal or pellet powered oven, aim to get the stone temperature to around 840°F (450°C), and then stop adding fuel so that the flames begin to die down. Once the flames are low (or have even died down completely) and the stone temperature has reduced to 750 to 790°F (400 to 420°C), give the peel a little shuffle/shake to ensure the dough isn't sticking. Launch your pizza confidently into the middle of your Ooni pizza oven and cook for 3 to 4 minutes, turning 90 degrees after approximately every minute. A good indication that the pizza is ready for the first turn is when the bottom of the pizza starts to form a rounded lip where it is in contact with the stone. To finish off the pizza, add a chunk of wood (or additional pellets) to the oven to spike the flames and cook for 1 to 2 minutes, turning regularly to achieve a nice, even bake. To make sure this chunk of wood ignites instantly, place it inside your oven directly on the stone (to one side so it isn't in the way) for 1 minute, so it warms up before using your peel to place it into the fuel tray from inside your oven.

Remove the pizza from the oven and slide it onto a cooling rack for 1 to 2 minutes before transferring to a display board. Evenly add oregano and cut into 6 slices. I like to make it look authentic by serving each slice on a paper plate. Add a generous drizzle of hot honey to finish.

DETROIT STYLE PIZZA

Cheese lovers gather around because you are not going to want to miss this chapter! The sight of a caramelized, crispy cheese wall (otherwise known as a frico) epitomizes the Detroit style pizza (DSP) and fills me with pure joy every time I release one from its pan. This frico, combined with a soft, pillow-like base and delicious toppings will have you smiling from ear to ear every time. The DSP is believed to have originated at Buddy's Rendezvous in Detroit in 1946, where they were baked in blue steel pans originally used for holding nuts and bolts in auto manufacturing plants. After making (and more importantly, eating) your first DSP, I'm pretty sure, like me, you'll be forever grateful to Buddy's Rendezvous!

You will notice that in all the recipes in this chapter I par-bake the dough without any toppings. This is to allow the dough to rise without being weighed down by toppings, resulting in a much lighter, airier dough. You will also achieve a wonderfully crisp bottom.

In this chapter, I am going to blow your mind with some seriously epic flavors. We're talking classic flavor pairings like Buffalo Chicken and Blue Cheese (page 121) as well as a recipe based around a British pub classic using pineapple cooked in rendered bacon fat (Hunter's Chicken on page 125). I told you they were epic!

Note: Throughout this chapter you will see me referring to pan grippers when removing the pan from the oven and holding the pan while removing the cooked pizza. These provide a safe way to handle the pan when hot. They can be easily found online.

CLASSIC RED TOP WITH A CREAMY TWIST

YIELD: 1 pizza (serves 2-3)

For the Sauce

1 full portion Keep-It-Simple Tomato Sauce (page 35)

1 tsp oregano

1 tsp garlic powder

16 g (1 tbsp) tomato puree

1 tbsp (15 ml) extra virgin olive oil

For the Pizza

1 (370-g) ball Detroit Dough (page 27)

261 g (2⅓ cups) freshly grated low-moisture mozzarella, divided

½ tbsp (8 ml) extra virgin olive oil

37 g (⅓ cup) grated Cheddar cheese

1 burrata ball

Drizzle of hot honey

Handful of chopped basil

There was only one way I could start this chapter, and that's with a true heavyweight in the Detroit pizza world: the classic Red Top! Named because its two iconic "racing stripes" of rich tomato sauce added on top of the cheese, this pizza (with or without my creamy twist), must be added to your pizza bucket list. While simple in terms of baking, as only cheese is added to the base pre-bake, the resulting flavors and textures are anything but simple. In fact, I'd go as far as to say they will be right at the top of the best you've ever had! The traditional Red Top consists of just two main toppings (cheese and sauce), so as this recipe title suggests, I've given it a "creamy twist" by adding fresh burrata as a post-bake topping. There will be traditionalists out there who say you should never tamper with a classic, and while I absolutely love a classic Red Top, adding burrata, hot honey and basil takes this pizza to a whole new level.

Fire up your Ooni pizza oven, and aim for a stone temperature of 750 to 790°F (400 to 420°C). Depending on the outside temperature, this should take approximately 15 to 20 minutes. In the colder months, an extra 10 to 15 minutes might be needed. You can check the stone temperature with an infrared thermometer.

While your Ooni pizza oven is heating up, pour a full portion of the sauce into a saucepan over low heat. While stirring, add the oregano, garlic powder, tomato puree and oil. Simmer for 10 minutes.

When the stone temperature has reached approximately 715°F (380°C), uncover the dough and evenly place 30 grams (⅓ cup) of the grated mozzarella around the four sides where the dough meets the pan. This will help prevent the dough from shrinking during the par-bake. Cover the pan with foil, and using heatproof oven gloves, place it into the center of your Ooni pizza oven. Cook using a medium flame for 6 minutes, turning once halfway through. Remove the foil and cook using a low flame for 3 to 4 minutes at the front of the oven, turning regularly to achieve a nice, even bake.

Remove the base from the pan (you may need to use a metal spatula to release it from the sides), and allow it to cool on a cooling rack. You can continue without cooling, but in my experience, letting it cool first makes it easier, once fully cooked, to release the cheese from the sides of the pan, helping to achieve that iconic cheese crown (frico).

(continued)

CLASSIC RED TOP WITH A CREAMY TWIST (CONTINUED)

Fire your Ooni pizza oven back up, this time aiming for a stone temperature of 680 to 720°F (360 to 380°C). Add the oil to the pan and spread it around the bottom and the sides with your fingers. Place the base back into the pan and add 180 grams (1⅔ cups) of the mozzarella around all four sides and corners. The key here is to try and build up a wall of cheese so that when it melts it sticks to the sides of the pan. This will seem like A LOT of cheese, but trust me, it will be worth it! Cover the rest of the base with the remaining mozzarella and Cheddar cheese.

Using heatproof oven gloves, place the pan into the front of your Ooni pizza oven and cook using a low to medium flame for 6 to 8 minutes, turning regularly to achieve a nice, even bake.

Remove the pan from the oven and place it onto a cooling rack, allowing it to cool for 4 to 5 minutes. While the pizza is cooling, warm up the tomato sauce. Use the pan grippers to hold the pan, while very carefully releasing the cheese from the sides of the pan with a metal spatula. Start at one end by very carefully sliding the metal spatula down behind the cheese (trying not to break any of it off), and then slowly sliding the spatula along the length of the pan until you reach the opposite end. Repeat this process for the remaining sides.

Remove the pizza from the pan and with a spoon or ladle, add 2 vertical stripes of tomato sauce along the length of the pizza. Add 4 or 6 (depending on how many pieces you are going cut the pizza into) dollops of burrata before adding a generous drizzle of hot honey and a sprinkle of chopped basil. Cut into 4 or 6 pieces and serve.

BUFFALO CHICKEN AND BLUE CHEESE

YIELD: 1 pizza (serves 2-3)

For the Blue Cheese Sauce

1 tbsp (14 g) butter

120 ml (½ cup) heavy cream (double cream)

68 g (½ cup) chopped blue cheese

Handful of chopped chives

For the Pizza

1 (370-g) ball Detroit Dough (page 27)

298 g (2⅔ cups) freshly grated low-moisture mozzarella, divided

½ tbsp (8 ml) extra virgin olive oil

3-4 chicken wings cooked in Buffalo sauce and pulled apart into small pieces

2 tbsp (30 ml) Buffalo sauce, plus extra for topping

Handful of chopped chives

An incredibly popular bar snack, fiery-hot Buffalo chicken wings and creamy, tangy blue cheese are a food pairing that dreams are made of. There aren't many other combinations in the world that pack as much flavor as this, and like anything else, using them as pizza toppings elevates them to new heights. I'll be honest, when it comes to spice and heat, my taste buds can't handle too much, but the creamy blue cheese works wonders in this recipe, leaving just enough heat to get your taste buds tingling. If you're a blue cheese lover like me, I recommend having a bowl of the rich and creamy sauce alongside this pizza to dunk into before each bite! If blue cheese isn't your thing, then a really good alternative is a nice, cool yogurt mint sauce.

Fire up your Ooni pizza oven, and aim for a stone temperature of 750 to 790°F (400 to 420°C). Depending on the outside temperature, this should take approximately 15 to 20 minutes. In the colder months, an extra 10 to 15 minutes might be needed. You can check the stone temperature with an infrared thermometer.

While your Ooni pizza oven is heating up, make the cheese sauce. Place the butter in a saucepan over a medium heat. Once melted, add the cream and simmer for 2 to 4 minutes, stirring frequently until it begins to thicken. Add the blue cheese and chives, and continue to simmer until the cheese starts to break down slightly. Take the sauce off the heat, pour into a container and set aside.

When the stone temperature has reached approximately 715°F (380°C), uncover the dough and evenly place 30 grams (⅓ cup) of the grated mozzarella around the four sides where the dough meets the pan. This will help prevent the dough from shrinking during the par-bake. Cover the pan with foil, and using heatproof oven gloves, place it into the center of your Ooni pizza oven. Cook using a medium flame for 6 minutes, turning once halfway through. Remove the foil and cook using a low flame for 3 to 4 minutes at the front of the oven, turning regularly to achieve a nice, even bake.

Remove the base from the pan (you may need to use a metal spatula to release it from the sides), and allow it to cool on a cooling rack. You can continue without cooling, but in my experience, letting it cool first makes it easier, once fully cooked, to release the cheese from the sides of the pan, helping to achieve that iconic cheese crown (frico).

(continued)

BUFFALO CHICKEN AND BLUE CHEESE (CONTINUED)

Fire your Ooni pizza oven back up, this time aiming for a stone temperature of 680 to 720°F (360 to 380°C). Add the oil to the pan and spread it around the bottom and the sides with your fingers. Place the base back into the pan and add 180 grams (1⅔ cups) of the mozzarella around all four sides and corners. The key here is to try and build up a wall of cheese so that when it melts it sticks to the sides of the pan. This will seem like A LOT of cheese, but trust me, it will be worth it! Cover the rest of the base with the remaining mozzarella before adding the Buffalo chicken pieces and Buffalo sauce.

Using heatproof oven gloves, place the pan into the front of your Ooni pizza oven and cook using a low to medium flame for 6 to 8 minutes, turning regularly to achieve a nice, even bake. Remove the pan from the oven and place it onto a cooling rack, allowing it to cool for 4 to 5 minutes. Use the pan grippers to hold the pan, while very carefully releasing the cheese from the sides of the pan with a metal spatula. Start at one end by very carefully sliding the metal spatula down behind the cheese (trying not to break any of it off), and then slowly sliding the spatula along the length of the pan until you reach the opposite end. Repeat this process for the remaining sides.

Remove the pizza from the pan and drizzle on some extra Buffalo sauce, ¼ cup (60 ml) of the blue cheese sauce and a sprinkling of the fresh chives. Cut into 4 or 6 pieces and serve.

HUNTER'S CHICKEN

YIELD: 1 pizza (serves 2-3)

100 g uncooked bacon or pancetta strips

54 g (⅓ cup) sliced fresh pineapple

1 (370-g) ball Detroit Dough (page 27)

298 g (2⅔ cups) freshly grated
low-moisture mozzarella, divided

½ tbsp (8 ml) extra virgin olive oil

1 cooked chicken breast (covered in
barbecue sauce), cut into small pieces

3 tbsp (45 ml) barbecue sauce

Handful of chopped coriander or cilantro

Hunter's chicken is a British pub classic that typically consists of a chicken breast wrapped in bacon, which is then smothered with barbecue sauce and cheese. I have always loved how these flavors work together, so after having it for a family dinner one evening, I knew I needed to get these ingredients onto a Detroit pizza. Due to the amount of cheese used for this style of pizza, I knew it would benefit from some additional sweetness to help cut through that richness. That something is not just pineapple, but pineapple cooked and charred in rendered bacon fat! This helps to marry all the flavors together. I'm big believer in the saying, "If something is worth doing, it is worth doing properly."

Fire up your Ooni pizza oven, and aim for a stone temperature of 750 to 790°F (400 to 420°C). Depending on the outside temperature, this should take approximately 15 to 20 minutes. In the colder months, an extra 10 to 15 minutes might be needed. You can check the stone temperature with an infrared thermometer.

While your Ooni pizza oven is heating up, cook the bacon in a skillet/frying pan over a medium heat until crispy. Remove the bacon from the skillet/frying pan, leaving the rendered fat in the pan, and set aside. Turn the heat up to high and loosen any bits off the bottom of the skillet/frying pan. (This is where all the flavor is.) Place the pineapple slices in the skillet/frying pan and cook in the rendered fat for 1 to 2 minutes on each side. Once nicely charred, remove from the skillet/frying pan and cut into small pieces ready for topping.

When the stone temperature has reached approximately 715°F (380°C), uncover the dough and evenly place 30 grams (⅓ cup) of the grated mozzarella around the four sides where the dough meets the pan. This will help prevent the dough from shrinking during the par-bake. Cover the pan with foil, and using heatproof oven gloves, place it into the center of your Ooni pizza oven. Cook using a medium flame for 6 minutes, turning once halfway through. Remove the foil and cook using a low flame for 3 to 4 minutes at the front of the oven, turning regularly to achieve a nice, even bake.

Remove the base from the pan (you may need to use a metal spatula to release it from the sides), and allow it to cool on a cooling rack. You can continue without cooling, but in my experience, letting it cool first makes it easier, once fully cooked, to release the cheese from the sides of the pan, helping to achieve that iconic cheese crown (frico).

(continued)

HUNTER'S CHICKEN (CONTINUED)

Fire your Ooni pizza oven back up, this time aiming for a stone temperature of 680 to 720°F (360 to 380°C). Add the oil to the pan and spread it around the bottom and the sides with your fingers. Place the base back into the pan and add 180 grams (1⅔ cups) of the mozzarella around all four sides and corners. The key here is to try and build up a wall of cheese so that when it melts it sticks to the sides of the pan. This will seem like A LOT of cheese, but trust me, it will be worth it! Cover the rest of the base with the remaining mozzarella, the chicken, bacon and pineapple.

Using heatproof oven gloves, place the pan into the front of your Ooni pizza oven and cook using a low to medium flame for 6 to 8 minutes, turning regularly to achieve a nice, even bake. Remove the pan from the oven and place it onto a cooling rack, allowing it to cool for 4 to 5 minutes. Use the pan grippers to hold the pan, while very carefully releasing the cheese from the sides of the pan with a metal spatula. Start at one end by very carefully sliding the metal spatula down behind the cheese (trying not to break any of it off), and then slowly sliding the spatula along the length of the pan until you reach the opposite end. Repeat this process for the remaining sides.

Remove the pizza from the pan and add a generous drizzle of barbecue sauce and a sprinkle of coriander. Cut into 4 or 6 pieces and serve.

VEGGIE HOT!

YIELD: 1 pizza (serves 2-3)

90 g (⅔ cup) baby corn

1 (370-g) ball Detroit Dough (page 27)

298 g (2⅔ cups) freshly grated low-moisture mozzarella, divided

½ tbsp (8 ml) extra virgin olive oil

1-2 medium tomatoes, thinly sliced

1-2 any type of chilies, thinly sliced (choose depending on the heat you desire)

This pizza is loaded with a beautiful combination of fresh flavors! When I think of a veggie pizza, I always picture peppers, mushrooms and tomatoes. While these are all great to use on a pizza, I didn't want to go down the traditional route with this recipe. Instead, I've opted for chilies, baby corn and a variety of tomatoes. Not only do these toppings give a beautiful, vibrant look to the pizza, but they also provide a knockout flavor that cuts through the richness of the creamy caramelized cheese. So, whether you're a vegetarian or not, be sure to give this recipe a go, so you too can experience its fresh flavors.

Fire up your Ooni pizza oven, and aim for a stone temperature of 750 to 790°F (400 to 420°C). Depending on the outside temperature, this should take approximately 15 to 20 minutes. In the colder months, an extra 10 to 15 minutes might be needed. You can check the stone temperature with an infrared thermometer.

While your Ooni pizza oven is heating up, bring a saucepan of lightly salted water to a boil. Reduce to a simmer, tip in the baby corn and cook for 4 to 5 minutes. Remove the corn and allow it to cool. Cut each piece of corn in half lengthways and set aside.

When the stone temperature has reached approximately 715°F (380°C), uncover the dough and evenly place 30 grams (⅓ cup) of the grated mozzarella around the four sides where the dough meets the pan. This will help prevent the dough from shrinking during the par-bake. Cover the pan with foil and using heatproof oven gloves, place it into the center of your Ooni pizza oven. Cook using a medium flame for 6 minutes, turning once halfway through. Remove the foil and cook using a low flame for 3 to 4 minutes at the front of the oven, turning regularly to achieve a nice, even bake.

Remove the base from the pan (you may need to use a metal spatula to release it from the sides), and allow it to cool on a cooling rack. You can continue without cooling, but in my experience, letting it cool first makes it easier, once fully cooked, to release the cheese from the sides of the pan, helping to achieve that iconic cheese crown (frico).

(continued)

VEGGIE HOT! (CONTINUED)

Fire your Ooni pizza oven back up, this time aiming for a stone temperature of 680 to 720°F (360 to 380°C). Add the oil to the pan and spread it around the bottom and the sides with your fingers. Place the base back into the pan and add 180 grams (1⅔ cups) of the mozzarella around all four sides and corners. The key here is to try and build up a wall of cheese so that when it melts it sticks to the sides of the pan. This will seem like A LOT of cheese, but trust me, it will be worth it! Cover the rest of the base with the remaining mozzarella before adding the tomatoes, baby corn and sliced chilies on top.

Using heatproof oven gloves, place the pan into the front of your Ooni pizza oven and cook using a low to medium flame for 6 to 8 minutes, turning regularly to achieve a nice, even bake. Remove the pan from the oven and place it onto a cooling rack, allowing it to cool for 4 to 5 minutes. Use the pan grippers to hold the pan, while very carefully releasing the cheese from the sides of the pan with a metal spatula. Start at one end by very carefully sliding the metal spatula down behind the cheese (trying not to break any of it off), and then slowly sliding the spatula along the length of the pan until you reach the opposite end. Repeat this process for the remaining sides. Remove the pizza from the pan, cut into 4 or 6 pieces and serve.

SOUTH AFRICAN BRAAI

YIELD: 1 pizza (serves 2-3)

For the Sauce

1 full portion of Keep-It-Simple Tomato Sauce (page 35)

15 ml (1 tbsp) barbecue sauce

1 tsp oregano

1 tsp garlic powder

16 g (1 tbsp) tomato puree

15 ml (1 tbsp) extra virgin olive oil

For the Pizza

1 (370-g) ball Detroit Dough (page 27)

298 g (2⅔ cups) freshly grated low-moisture mozzarella, divided

½ tbsp (8 ml) extra virgin olive oil

1 boerewors sausage, chopped into slices

60 g roast lamb, cut into small pieces

3-4 chicken wings, pulled apart into small pieces

Handful of finely chopped biltong

Handful of pomegranate seeds

Handful of chopped coriander or cilantro

This is the ultimate meat lover's dream! Braai is the South African equivalent of a barbecue, and from my recent visits to this wonderful country, if there's one thing I took away, it was that South Africans love to barbecue! A braai, however, is more than just preparing and cooking meat; it's a social occasion with a joyful, happy atmosphere. This pizza is dedicated to my South African family, whom I must thank for introducing me to this special tradition and the wonderful local cuisine. For this recipe, I've opted to use lamb and chicken along with boerewors (a spicy, South African sausage) and biltong (a South African dried, cured meat similar to beef jerky). If you can't find these South African delicacies, this recipe is also perfect for using leftover barbecue meat, so you could use whatever meats you have left. Adding the fresh coriander and pomegranate post-bake gives this pizza a freshness and finishes it off perfectly.

Fire up your Ooni pizza oven, and aim for a stone temperature of 750 to 790°F (400 to 420°C). Depending on the outside temperature, this should take approximately 15 to 20 minutes. In the colder months, an extra 10 to 15 minutes might be needed. You can check the stone temperature with an infrared thermometer.

While your Ooni pizza oven is heating up, make the sauce by adding a full portion of the sauce, barbecue sauce, oregano, garlic powder, tomato puree and oil to a saucepan over low heat. Stir until combined, and simmer for 10 minutes. You can make the sauce a day ahead and store it in the fridge until required.

When the stone temperature has reached approximately 715°F (380°C), uncover the dough and evenly place 30 grams (⅓ cup) of the grated mozzarella around the four sides where the dough meets the pan. This will help prevent the dough from shrinking during the par-bake. Cover the pan with foil and using heatproof oven gloves, place it into the center of your Ooni pizza oven. Cook using a medium flame for 6 minutes, turning once halfway through. Remove the foil and cook using a low flame for 3 to 4 minutes at the front of the oven, turning regularly to achieve a nice, even bake.

Remove the base from the pan (you may need to use a metal spatula to release it from the sides), and allow it to cool on a cooling rack. You can continue without cooling, but in my experience, letting it cool first makes it easier, once fully cooked, to release the cheese from the sides of the pan, helping to achieve that iconic cheese crown (frico).

(continued)

SOUTH AFRICAN BRAAI (CONTINUED)

Fire your Ooni pizza oven back up, this time aiming for a stone temperature of 680 to 720°F (360 to 380°C). Add the oil to the pan and spread it around the bottom and the sides with your fingers. Place the base back into the pan and add 180 grams (1⅔ cups) of the mozzarella around all four sides and corners. The key here is to try and build up a wall of cheese so that when it melts it sticks to the sides of the pan. This will seem like A LOT of cheese, but trust me, it will be worth it! Add ¼ cup (60 ml) of the sauce to the center of the par-baked base, and spread it out toward the four edges using the back of your spoon until you reach the edge of the cheese. Add the remaining mozzarella on top of the sauce before adding the boerewors sausage, lamb and chicken evenly across the top.

Using heatproof oven gloves, place the pan into the front of your Ooni pizza oven and cook using a low to medium flame for 6 to 8 minutes, turning regularly to achieve a nice, even bake. Remove the pan from the oven and place it onto a cooling rack, allowing it to cool for 4 to 5 minutes. Use the pan grippers to hold the pan, while very carefully releasing the cheese from the sides of the pan with a metal spatula. Start at one end by very carefully sliding the metal spatula down behind the cheese (trying not to break any of it off), and then slowly sliding the spatula along the length of the pan until you reach the opposite end. Repeat this process for the remaining sides.

Remove the pizza from the pan and finish by adding the biltong, pomegranate seeds and coriander. Cut into 4 or 6 pieces and serve.

TONDA ROMANA (THIN AND CRISPY ROMAN STYLE)

The Tonda Romana (tonda meaning "round") is a thin-crust pizza from Rome. The standout feature of this style of pizza is its cracker-like crust with charred air bubbles. Due to the high temperatures you can achieve in your Ooni pizza oven, these pockets of air will inflate seconds after you launch the pizza into the oven. Whenever I make this style of pizza, I always get excited at seeing this stage of the bake as it's a telltale sign that you got the fermentation of the dough spot-on. The more I make this style of pizza, the more I fall in love with it, and I am super excited to share my recipes so you too can experience this beautiful and traditional Italian style in the comfort of your own home.

I find that certain topping combinations are more suited to certain styles of pizza, so for this chapter, I have included a range of recipes I think suit the Tonda Romana style superbly. And if you're a cheese lover, you're not going to want to miss my Cheese, Cheese and More Cheese (page 137)!

CHEESE, CHEESE AND MORE CHEESE!

YIELD: 1 pizza (serves 1-2)

56 g (½ cup) fresh mozzarella

28 g (2 tbsp) ricotta

½ tsp lemon juice

Pinch of salt

1 (170-g) ball of Tonda Romana Dough (page 30)

56 g (½ cup) smoked scamorza, chopped into small pieces

Drizzle of extra virgin olive oil

Fine semolina flour

Black pepper, to taste

If you are a cheese lover like me, then this is the pizza for you. I chose to use mozzarella, lemon-infused ricotta and smoked scamorza in this recipe because they complement each other beautifully and each bring something special to the party. There are, however, so many other varieties of cheese in the world, meaning you can simply choose your favorites and put them together on top of your pizza base. Whatever you choose, I am extremely confident the result will be gooey, cheesy heaven! As the flavor profile of this pizza is very rich and creamy, I like to add lemon juice to the ricotta and finish with some cracked black pepper. Make sure you have a camera ready when you slice up this pizza, as I'm sure there will be an amazing cheese pull to capture!

To keep the pizza from getting soggy, remove as much moisture from the fresh mozzarella as possible. Do this by using a sharp knife to cut the mozzarella ball into very small cubes and laying them down onto a few layers of paper towels at least 1 hour before cooking. To help draw out even more moisture, lay another paper towel on top as well. I find that dicing the mozzarella rather than breaking it into pieces (like in my Neapolitan recipes) is better suited to this style of pizza.

In a small bowl, mix together the ricotta, lemon juice and salt. Set aside.

Fire up your Ooni pizza oven, and aim for a stone temperature of 715 to 750°F (380 to 400°C). Depending on the outside temperature, this should take approximately 15 to 20 minutes. In the colder months, an extra 10 to 15 minutes might be needed. You can check the stone temperature with an infrared thermometer.

When the stone has reached approximately 660°F (350°C), stretch out the dough ball using the instructions on page 33.

Add the mozzarella and scamorza evenly onto the dough, leaving a .2-inch (5-mm) border. Add small dollops of the lemon-infused ricotta in the small gaps between the pieces of mozzarella and scamorza to give a nice, uniform coverage. Add a drizzle of oil.

Give your chosen pizza peel a light dusting of semolina flour before transferring the dough onto it. You can do this by lying the peel flat alongside the dough, and then, using both hands, gently lift the edge of the dough and slide it onto the peel. This stage can be daunting, but be confident and do it in one smooth, quick movement. After sliding the dough onto the peel, give it a final reshape. If you don't feel confident enough to use this technique, you can place the stretched-out dough straight onto the floured peel after stretching it over your knuckles and top while it is on the peel.

(continued)

CHEESE, CHEESE AND MORE CHEESE! (CONTINUED)

When the stone temperature has reached 715 to 750°F (380 to 400°C), give the peel a little shuffle/shake to ensure the dough isn't sticking, and then launch confidently into the middle of your Ooni pizza oven. If you are using a gas-powered Ooni pizza oven, turn the flame down to medium. If your oven is pellet or wood/charcoal powered, try and time your launch so the flames aren't too fierce. Do not take your eyes off the pizza, as a few seconds can make a big difference to the overall bake!

After approximately 20 to 30 seconds, you will see air bubbles inflate all around the crust. When the air bubbles at the back of the oven start to brown/blister, warm the metal peel/turning peel in the back of the oven by holding it in the flames for a few seconds. (This will help stop the peel from sticking to the bottom of the pizza.) Then, carefully slide it under the pizza and turn it 180 degrees. When the air bubbles that are now at the back of the oven start to brown/blister, turn the pizza again, but this time, 90 degrees. Finally, do one last 180-degree turn so that all of the pizza has an even bake. The total cooking time should be approximately 2 to 2½ minutes.

Remove the pizza from the oven and slide it onto a cooling rack for 1 to 2 minutes before transferring to a display board. Finish by adding some black pepper. Cut into 6 slices and serve hot.

PROSCIUTTO AND CHILI JAM

YIELD: 1 pizza (serves 1-2)

56 g (½ cup) fresh mozzarella

1 (170-g) ball of Tonda Romana Dough (page 30)

2–3 tbsp (30–45 ml) Keep-It-Simple Tomato Sauce (page 35)

1 tsp finely grated Grana Padano

Drizzle of extra virgin olive oil

Fine semolina flour

25 g prosciutto

15 ml (1 tbsp) chili jam

Fresh basil leaves

Some foods pair so well together they create a harmonious marriage of flavors. Lamb with mint and chocolate with nuts are two prime examples of this, and you can now add prosciutto and chili jam to that list. This flavor pairing is right at the top of my favorite pizza topping combinations, and if you haven't tried it before, I'm so excited that it will be this recipe that introduces you to it. I have experimented by adding the prosciutto both pre- and post-bake, but for this pizza, I recommend using it post-bake. The silky texture of the uncooked prosciutto combines perfectly with the sweetness and heat of the chili jam. A key element of this pizza is achieving the right balance of toppings. Try and keep the pieces of prosciutto small so that you experience the combination of flavors and textures in each bite.

To keep the pizza from getting soggy, remove as much moisture from the fresh mozzarella as possible. Do this by using a sharp knife to cut the mozzarella ball into very small cubes and laying them down onto a few layers of paper towels at least 1 hour before cooking. To help draw out even more moisture, lay another paper towel on top as well. I find that dicing the mozzarella rather than breaking it into pieces (like in my Neapolitan recipes) is better suited to this style of pizza.

Fire up your Ooni pizza oven, and aim for a stone temperature of 715 to 750°F (380 to 400°C). Depending on the outside temperature, this should take approximately 15 to 20 minutes. In the colder months, an extra 10 to 15 minutes might be needed. You can check the stone temperature with an infrared thermometer.

When the stone has reached approximately 660°F (350°C), stretch out the dough ball using the instructions on page 33.

Add the tomato sauce to the center of the base and spread in a circular motion, moving out toward the edge using the back of your spoon, leaving a .2-inch (5-mm) border. Evenly add the Grana Padano and fresh mozzarella before a drizzle of oil.

Give your chosen pizza peel a light dusting of semolina flour before transferring the dough onto it. You can do this by lying the peel flat alongside the dough, and then, using both hands, gently lift the edge of the dough and slide it onto the peel. This stage can be daunting, but be confident and do it in one smooth, quick movement. After sliding the dough onto the peel, give it a final reshape. If you don't feel confident enough to use this technique, you can place the stretched-out dough straight onto the floured peel after stretching it over your knuckles and top while it is on the peel.

(continued)

PROSCIUTTO AND CHILI JAM (CONTINUED)

When the stone temperature has reached 715 to 750°F (380 to 400°C), give the peel a little shuffle/shake to ensure the dough isn't sticking, and then launch confidently into the middle of your Ooni pizza oven. If you are using a gas-powered Ooni pizza oven, turn the flame down to medium. If your oven is pellet or wood/charcoal powered, try and time your launch so the flames aren't too fierce. Do not take your eyes off the pizza, as a few seconds can make a big difference to the overall bake!

After approximately 20 to 30 seconds, you will see air bubbles inflate all around the crust. When the air bubbles at the back of the oven start to brown/blister, warm the metal peel/turning peel in the back of the oven by holding it in the flames for a few seconds. (This will help stop the peel from sticking to the bottom of the pizza.) Then, carefully slide it under the pizza and turn it 180 degrees. When the air bubbles that are now at the back of the oven start to brown/blister, turn the pizza again, but this time, 90 degrees. Finally, do one last 180-degree turn so that all of the pizza has an even bake. The total cooking time should be approximately 2 to 2½ minutes.

Remove the pizza from the oven and slide it onto a cooling rack for 1 to 2 minutes before transferring to a display board. Evenly add the prosciutto before adding small dollops of chili jam. The key here is to make sure there is enough chili jam so that each bite has a bit of that chili kick! Neatly add the fresh basil leaves to the center. Cut into 6 slices and serve hot.

THE PERFECT PEAR

YIELD: 1 pizza (serves 1-2)

56 g (½ cup) fresh mozzarella

1 (170-g) ball of Tonda Romana Dough (page 30)

10 g blue cheese, chopped into small pieces

1 pear, thinly sliced vertically*

Drizzle of extra virgin olive oil

Fine semolina flour

Handful of chopped walnuts

Drizzle of hot honey

* Slice as thinly as possible just before topping your pizza so the slices don't brown.

This pear, blue cheese and walnut pizza has such a well-balanced choice of toppings. The sweetness of the pear complements the strong flavor of the blue cheese perfectly. The crunch from the walnuts and bit of heat from the hot honey really does tick so many boxes on the flavor and texture charts! Before embarking on my pizza journey, blue cheese was something I only ate once a year, on Christmas day, along with some crackers and a glass of port. This is no longer the case! Blue cheese is something I'm regularly adding to various pizzas now. You do have to be careful with how much you use, as it is very easy to overpower the rest of the toppings, but once you achieve the right balance, the results will be mind-blowing.

To keep the pizza from getting soggy, remove as much moisture from the fresh mozzarella as possible. Do this by using a sharp knife to cut the mozzarella ball into very small cubes and laying them down onto a few layers of paper towels at least 1 hour before cooking. To help draw out even more moisture, lay another paper towel on top as well. I find that dicing the mozzarella rather than breaking it into pieces (like in my Neapolitan recipes) is better suited to this style of pizza.

Fire up your Ooni pizza oven, and aim for a stone temperature of 715 to 750°F (380 to 400°C). Depending on the outside temperature, this should take approximately 15 to 20 minutes. In the colder months, an extra 10 to 15 minutes might be needed. You can check the stone temperature with an infrared thermometer.

When the stone has reached approximately 660°F (350°C), stretch out the dough ball using the instructions on page 33.

Add the mozzarella and blue cheese evenly onto the dough, leaving a .2-inch (5-mm) border. Arrange the pear slices neatly on top of the cheese before a drizzle of oil.

Give your chosen pizza peel a light dusting of semolina flour before transferring the dough onto it. You can do this by lying the peel flat alongside the dough, and then, using both hands, gently lift the edge of the dough and slide it onto the peel. This stage can be daunting, but be confident and do it in one smooth, quick movement. After sliding the dough onto the peel, give it a final reshape. If you don't feel confident enough to use this technique, you can place the stretched-out dough straight onto the floured peel after stretching it over your knuckles and top while it is on the peel.

(continued)

THE PERFECT PEAR
(CONTINUED)

When the stone temperature has reached 715 to 750°F (380 to 400°C), give the peel a little shuffle/shake to ensure the dough isn't sticking, and then launch confidently into the middle of your Ooni pizza oven. If you are using a gas-powered Ooni pizza oven, turn the flame down to medium. If your oven is pellet or wood/charcoal powered, try and time your launch so the flames aren't too fierce. Do not take your eyes off the pizza, as a few seconds can make a big difference to the overall bake!

After approximately 20 to 30 seconds, you will see air bubbles inflate all around the crust. When the air bubbles at the back of the oven start to brown/blister, warm the metal peel/turning peel in the back of the oven by holding it in the flames for a few seconds. (This will help stop the peel from sticking to the bottom of the pizza.) Then, carefully slide it under the pizza and turn it 180 degrees. When the air bubbles that are now at the back of the oven start to brown/blister, turn the pizza again, but this time, 90 degrees. Finally, do one last 180-degree turn so that all of the pizza has an even bake. The total cooking time should be approximately 2 to 2½ minutes.

Remove the pizza from the oven and slide it onto a cooling rack for 1 to 2 minutes before transferring to a display board. Add the chopped walnuts and a drizzle of hot honey to finish. Cut into 6 slices and serve hot.

TASTY TAPAS PIZZA

YIELD: 1 pizza (serves 1-2)

For the Roasted Potatoes
1 potato
15 ml (1 tbsp) garlic oil
1 tsp salt

For the Pizza
56 g (½ cup) fresh mozzarella
1 (170-g) ball of Tonda Romana Dough (page 30)
2-3 tbsp (30-45 ml) Keep-It-Simple Tomato Sauce (page 35)
1 tsp finely grated Grana Padano
8-10 chorizo slices
Drizzle of extra virgin olive oil
Fine semolina flour
Fresh basil leaves

When I think of chorizo with roast potatoes, I imagine a tasty Spanish tapas dish. In my opinion, the only better way to use these two ingredients is together on top of a pizza! The crispy potatoes are infused with the savory oils released from the chorizo while inside your Ooni pizza oven. Finished off with a touch of freshness from the basil, this is a pizza that I'm confident you will be making more than once. Another reason why I love this recipe is that it's another pizza that includes roasted potatoes. As unusual as it may sound, potato on pizza works incredibly well and is very popular in Italy. If you're treating yourself to some carbs, you might as well do it properly and go all out with "carbs on carbs for the win!"

Preheat your home oven to 400°F (200°C).

I recommend making the potatoes the day before and keeping them in the fridge until needed. While the oven is heating up, peel and slice the potato as thinly as possible before parboiling for 3 to 4 minutes. Drain the potatoes in a colander or sieve. As these are thin, do not shake them or they will break. Place the slices of potato onto a baking tray and pour the garlic oil evenly on top. Sprinkle the salt over the potatoes before roasting for 15 to 20 minutes. It's important not to cook the potatoes for too long as they will be added to the pizza pre-bake and cooked further in Ooni pizza oven. As soon as the potatoes start to brown around the edges, remove them from the oven. Set aside.

To keep the pizza from getting soggy, remove as much moisture from the fresh mozzarella as possible. Do this by using a sharp knife to cut the mozzarella ball into very small cubes and laying them down onto a few layers of paper towels at least 1 hour before cooking. To help draw out even more moisture, lay another paper towel on top as well. I find that dicing the mozzarella rather than breaking it into pieces (like in my Neapolitan recipes) is better suited to this style of pizza.

Fire up your Ooni pizza oven, and aim for a stone temperature of 715 to 750°F (380 to 400°C). Depending on the outside temperature, this should take approximately 15 to 20 minutes. In the colder months, an extra 10 to 15 minutes might be needed. You can check the stone temperature with an infrared thermometer.

When the stone has reached approximately 660°F (350°C), stretch out the dough ball using the instructions on page 33.

(continued)

TASTY TAPAS PIZZA (CONTINUED)

Add the tomato sauce to the center of the base and spread in a circular motion, moving out toward the edge using the back of your spoon, leaving a .2-inch (5-mm) border. Evenly add the Grana Padano and fresh mozzarella. Alternate adding slices of the roast potato and chorizo, overlapping each slice to give a neat fan effect. Drizzle some oil evenly over the base. It is important to leave the roast potatoes in the fridge right up until this point, as keeping them cold will help prevent them from charring too much under the flames in your Ooni pizza oven.

Give your chosen pizza peel a light dusting of semolina flour before transferring the dough onto it. You can do this by lying the peel flat alongside the dough, and then, using both hands, gently lift the edge of the dough and slide it onto the peel. This stage can be daunting, but be confident and do it in one smooth, quick movement. After sliding the dough onto the peel, give it a final reshape. If you don't feel confident enough to use this technique, you can place the stretched-out dough straight onto the floured peel after stretching it over your knuckles and top while it is on the peel.

When the stone temperature has reached 715 to 750°F (380 to 400°C), give the peel a little shuffle/shake to ensure the dough isn't sticking, and then launch confidently into the middle of your Ooni pizza oven. If you are using a gas-powered Ooni pizza oven, turn the flame down to medium. If your oven is pellet or wood/charcoal powered, try and time your launch so the flames aren't too fierce. Do not take your eyes off the pizza, as a few seconds can make a big difference to the overall bake!

After approximately 20 to 30 seconds, you will see air bubbles inflate all around the crust. When the air bubbles at the back of the oven start to brown/blister, warm the metal peel/turning peel in the back of the oven by holding it in the flames for a few seconds. (This will help stop the peel from sticking to the bottom of the pizza.) Then, carefully slide it under the pizza and turn it 180 degrees. When the air bubbles that are now at the back of the oven start to brown/blister, turn the pizza again, but this time, 90 degrees. Finally, do one last 180-degree turn so that all of the pizza has an even bake. The total cooking time should be approximately 2 to 2½ minutes.

Remove the pizza from the oven and slide it onto a cooling rack for 1 to 2 minutes before transferring to a display board. Finish by evenly adding the chopped basil. Cut into 6 slices and serve hot.

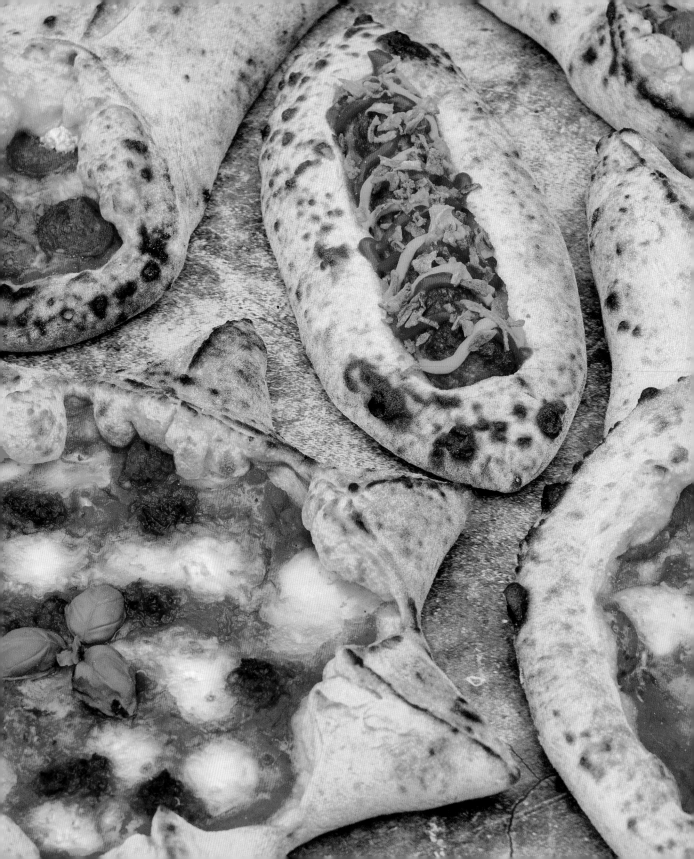

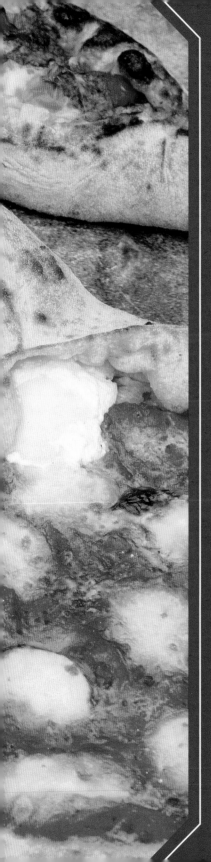

SOMETHING A BIT DIFFERENT

I really enjoy stepping outside the box when it comes to making pizzas. It truly amazes me how versatile one single ball of dough can be, and I'm so excited to be able to share some of my favorite shaped pizzas with you in this chapter. These are all great to make if you want to wow your pizza party guests, and they are always a hit with kids.

In this chapter, you will find a wide variety of different shapes and styles of pizza, all of which have two main things in common: They are all super-fun to make, and they are all incredibly delicious! So, whether you're making my Garlic Dough Strips (page 167) or my dog-bone-shaped Pizza Cannolo (page 159), you'll have a big smile on your face and a satisfied stomach. Most of these recipes are a little bit more involved when it comes to stretching and shaping the dough, but don't worry, I've got you covered with all the tips and tricks you'll need, along with some helpful step-by-step photos.

PIZZA RACCHETTA (AKA THE TENNIS RACKET PIZZA)

YIELD: 1 pizza (serves 1-2)

74 g (⅔ cup) fresh mozzarella, divided
1 (275-g) ball Neapolitan Dough (page 19)
16 g (1 tbsp) ricotta

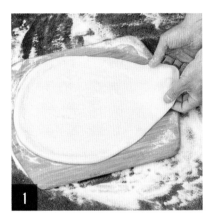

What is a pizza racchetta? In Italian, the word *racchetta* means "racket," so very simply, it's a pizza shaped like a tennis racket. This is a super-fun pizza to make, which combines a cheesy calzone "handle" with a beautiful Margherita "head." I decided to keep the toppings very simple here, as the focus needs to be on shaping the dough. But once mastered, you can use whatever toppings and fillings your heart desires. To make sure that the dough that forms the "handle" of this pizza is cooked through, you'll notice I've reduced the target temperature slightly inside your Ooni pizza oven and increased the cooking time to approximately 90 seconds. If you are sharing this pizza, you've got a big decision to make . . . are you going for the handle or the head?

To keep the pizza from getting soggy, remove as much moisture from the fresh mozzarella as possible by breaking it into small pieces and laying them down onto a few layers of paper towels at least 1 hour before cooking. To help draw out even more moisture, lay another paper towel on top as well.

Fire up your Ooni pizza oven, and aim for a stone temperature of 715 to 750°F (380 to 400°C). Depending on the outside temperature, this should take approximately 15 to 20 minutes. In the colder months, an extra 10 to 15 minutes might be needed. You can check the stone temperature with an infrared thermometer.

When the stone has reached approximately 660°F (350°C), stretch out the dough ball using the instructions on page 21.

Using your fingertips, flatten the bottom third of the crust you have formed. (This will be made into the tennis racket "handle.") Carefully lift the bottom of the dough (in the middle of the section you have just flattened), and gently pull this toward you to make the dough into a teardrop shape (refer to photo 1).

Add the ricotta and 30 grams (¼ cup) of the mozzarella to the middle of the section of dough you pulled toward you. Create the "handle" by lifting both sides of the dough (either side of the ricotta and mozzarella) until they meet in the center, and pinch together to create a seal, stopping when you get to where the crust that was not flattened begins (refer to photo 2).

(continued)

PIZZA RACCHETTA (CONTINUED)

1-2 tbsp (30 ml) Keep-It-Simple Tomato Sauce (page 35)

Fresh basil leaves, soaked in salt water*

1 tsp finely grated Grana Padano

Drizzle of extra virgin olive oil

Fine semolina flour

* Soaking the basil leaves in salt water protects them from burning, since they are added before baking.

Add the tomato sauce to the center of the base (the tennis racket "head") and spread in a circular motion, moving out toward the crust using the back of your spoon. Add the basil leaves, Grana Padano, the remaining mozzarella and a drizzle of oil (refer to photo 3).

Give your chosen pizza peel a light dusting of semolina flour before transferring the dough onto it. Make sure that the "handle" is at the back of the peel as we want this to be at the front of the oven first. You can do this by lying the peel flat alongside the dough, and then, using both hands, gently lift the edge of the dough and slide it onto the peel. This stage can be daunting, but be confident and do it in one smooth, quick movement. After sliding the dough onto the peel, give it a final reshape. If you don't feel confident enough to use this technique, you can place the stretched-out dough straight onto the floured peel after stretching it over your knuckles and shape and top while it is on the peel.

When the stone temperature has reached 715 to 750°F (380 to 400°C), give the peel a little shuffle/shake to ensure the dough isn't sticking, and then launch confidently into the middle of your Ooni pizza oven.

After approximately 20 seconds, you will begin to see the crust at the back of the oven start to brown/blister. At this point, warm the metal peel/turning peel in the back of the oven by holding it in the flames for a few seconds. (This will help stop the peel from sticking to the bottom of the pizza.) Then, carefully slide it under the pizza and turn it 180 degrees. When the "handle" that is now at the back of the oven starts to brown/blister, turn the pizza again, but this time, 90 degrees. Finally, do one last 180-degree turn so that all the pizza has an even bake. The total cooking time should be approximately 90 seconds.

Remove the pizza from the oven and slide it onto a cooling rack for 1 to 2 minutes before transferring to a display board. Cut and serve hot. I like to cut the "handle" off and tear it up to show off all of the gooey cheese inside.

TRIPLE CHEESE AND HAM CALZONE

YIELD: 1 calzone (serves 1-2)

56 g (½ cup) fresh mozzarella

1 (275-g) ball Neapolitan Dough (page 19)

Fine semolina flour

56 g (½ cup) freshly grated low-moisture mozzarella

56 g (½ cup) grated Cheddar cheese

30 g ham, cut into small cubes

1–2 tbsp (15–30 ml) Keep-It-Simple Tomato Sauce (page 35), plus extra for serving

Fresh basil leaves

I've made a lot of great calzones with some interesting fillings but this is the one that stands out for me. The inspiration for making this comes from my love for an uncomplicated cheese and ham sandwich. So, I've simply replaced the slices of bread with pizza dough. When cooking a calzone in your Ooni pizza oven, it is important to do so at a slightly lower temperature of 660 to 750°F (350 to 400°C). As the dough is folded over, concealing the fillings, it requires a longer bake compared to other pizzas. Cooking at a higher temperature will result in a burnt outside with an undercooked center.

To keep the calzone from getting soggy, remove as much moisture from the fresh mozzarella as possible by breaking it into small pieces and laying them down onto a few layers of paper towels at least 1 hour before cooking. To help draw out even more moisture, lay another paper towel on top as well.

When your dough ball has rested for 4 to 6 hours at room temperature (or 3 hours after removing it from the fridge), fire up your Ooni pizza oven, aiming for a stone temperature of 660 to 750°F (350 to 400°C). Depending on the outside temperature, this should take approximately 15 to 20 minutes. In the colder months, an extra 10 to 15 minutes might be needed. You can check the stone temperature with an infrared thermometer.

When the stone temperature has reached approximately 610°F (320°C), tip out your dough ball from the container (or remove it from the dough tray) onto a bed of fine semolina flour. (If you don't have fine semolina, you can use normal 00 flour that you used to make your dough.) Cover the ball with some extra semolina so the whole dough is coated and not sticky to the touch. If the dough has lost its circular shape, reshape it at this point. From the center, using your fingers, carefully push the dough down and out, going all the way to the edge. Do not leave any crust (refer to photo 1 in Tonda Romana dough recipe on page 33).

Keep rotating the dough as you do this to maintain its circular shape as this will impact the final shape of your calzone once it is cooked. Flip the dough over and continue to stretch it out using this technique. Once the dough has been stretched as far as possible using this technique, pick the dough up and carefully toss it from one hand to the other a few times to remove some of the excess flour. Hang the dough up right over both sets of your knuckles and rotate the dough through your hands, allowing gravity to stretch it out (refer to photo 6 in Neapolitan dough recipe on page 21).

(continued)

TRIPLE CHEESE AND
HAM CALZONE (CONTINUED)

Make sure it is the outer edge that hangs off your knuckles. It's important not to stretch from the center as this will make the base too thin, causing it to tear. Once the dough is evenly stretched to about 9 inches (23 cm), place it down straight onto a floured peel. As you will be forming the shape and topping directly on a peel, I recommend using a little bit more flour on the peel to make sure it doesn't stick.

The reason we make this a little smaller than the other Neapolitan recipes is to make the base a little thicker. This reduces the likelihood of it tearing under the additional weight of the toppings. Using your fingertips, gently press down around the edge to make sure it is nice and flat (refer to photo 1).

Add the fresh mozzarella (reserving a few small pieces for later), low-moisture mozzarella, Cheddar and diced ham to one half of the dough, leaving a 1-inch (2.5-cm) gap around the edge (refer to photo 2).

Lift the dough from the back, and pull it over the fillings before lining up the edges. At this point, if you feel like there is too much dough around the edge to be sealed, use a pizza cutter to trim off a section (refer to photo 3).

Pinch all the way around the edge to seal the top and bottom together (refer to photo 4).

Pierce a small hole in the top of the dough, which will allow the steam to escape during the bake so that it doesn't overinflate and burn. Add the tomato sauce to the top of the calzone, and carefully spread it using the back of a spoon before adding small pieces of the remaining fresh mozzarella (refer to photo 5).

When the stone temperature has reached of 660 to 750°F (350 to 400°C), give the peel a little shuffle/shake to ensure the dough isn't sticking, and then launch confidently into the middle of your Ooni pizza oven. Do not take your eyes off the calzone, as a few seconds can make a big difference to the overall bake!

After approximately 30 to 45 seconds you will see the back of the calzone start to brown/blister. Warm the metal peel/turning peel in the back of the oven by holding it in the flames for a few seconds. (This will help stop the peel from sticking to the bottom of the dough.) Then, carefully slide it under the calzone and turn it 180 degrees. When the side of the calzone at the back of the oven starts to brown/blister, turn it again, but this time, 90 degrees. Finally, do one last 180-degree turn so that all the calzone has an even bake. The total cooking time should be approximately 2 to 3 minutes. If at any point during the bake the calzone is starting to burn, move it as far away from the direct flame as possible.

Remove the calzone from the oven and slide onto a cooling rack for 1 to 2 minutes before transferring to a display board. Neatly add the fresh basil leaves to the top of the calzone to finish. Cut in half to admire all of that melted cheese and serve hot with a side of Keep-It-Simple Tomato Sauce.

ALL ABOARD THE TURKISH PIDE

YIELD: 2 pides (serves 1-2)

56 g (½ cup) fresh mozzarella
200 g (1⅓ cups) cherry tomatoes
Drizzle of extra virgin olive oil
1 tsp sea salt
1 (275-g) ball Neapolitan Dough (page 19)
Fine semolina flour
1 tsp green pesto

A Turkish Pide is a boat-shaped flatbread that is traditionally topped with various fillings (with spiced mincemeat a favorite) and cooked in a clay or stone oven. I've put my own spin on it by using some classic pizza flavors and switched out the traditional flatbread for my Neapolitan dough. The roasted cherry tomatoes, mozzarella and pesto all encased by a light fluffy Neapolitan dough make this the perfect comfort food. Shaping and assembling this pide is a little bit more involved than a standard pizza, but by following my step-by-step instructions, you'll be smiling from ear to ear when you take this out of your Ooni pizza oven.

To keep the pide from getting soggy, remove as much moisture from the fresh mozzarella as possible by breaking it into small pieces and laying them down onto a few layers of paper towels at least 1 hour before cooking. To help draw out even more moisture, lay another paper towel on top as well.

Preheat your home oven to 400°F (200°C).

Cut the cherry tomatoes in half, and place them on a baking tray. Drizzle the oil over the tomatoes and add the salt. Roast for 15 to 20 minutes, or until they break down. Remove the tomatoes from the oven and set aside to cool.

When your dough ball has rested for 4 to 6 hours at room temperature (or 3 hours after removing it from the fridge), fire up your Ooni pizza oven, aiming for a stone temperature of 715 to 750°F (380 to 400°C). Depending on the outside temperature, this should take approximately 15 to 20 minutes. In the colder months, an extra 10 to 15 minutes might be needed. You can check the stone temperature with an infrared thermometer.

When the stone temperature has reached approximately 660°F (350°C), tip out your dough ball from the container (or remove it from the dough tray) onto a bed of fine semolina flour. (If you don't have fine semolina, you can use normal 00 flour that you used to make your dough.) Cover the ball with some extra semolina so the whole dough is coated and not sticky to the touch. If the dough has lost its circular shape, reshape it at this point. Using a dough cutter, cut the dough ball in half and form each half into oval shapes (refer to photo 1). Set aside 1 of the halves for a second pide.

Take one of the halves and, from the bottom, using your fingers, carefully push the dough down and out, going all the way to the top. Do not leave any crust (refer to photo 2).

(continued)

ALL ABOARD THE TURKISH PIDE (CONTINUED)

Flip the dough over and repeat this technique on the other side. With a rolling pin, roll out the dough evenly until your oval is approximately 5 x 10 inches (13 x 25 cm). Pick the dough up and carefully toss it from one hand to the other a few times to remove some of the excess flour before placing it down horizontally onto a floured peel. As you will be forming the shape and topping directly on a peel, I recommend using a little bit more flour on the peel to make sure it doesn't stick.

Add the roasted tomatoes, mozzarella and pesto to the center of the dough (refer to photo 3).

Starting at one end, lift the two sides of the dough until they meet in the center, and pinch together to create a seal, stopping approximately 2 to 3 inches (5–8 cm) from the end. Repeat this at the other end (refer to photo 4).

At this point, you may need to neaten up the central opening of the pide if it has lost its shape. We are aiming for a pointed oval shape (refer to photo 5).

When the stone temperature has reached 715 to 750°F (380 to 400°C), give the peel a little shuffle/shake to ensure the dough isn't sticking, and then launch confidently into the middle of your Ooni pizza oven. Do not take your eyes off the pide, as a few seconds can make a big difference to the overall bake!

After approximately 20 to 30 seconds you will begin to see the top of the pide at the back of the oven start to brown/blister. Warm the metal peel/turning peel in the back of the oven by holding it in the flames for a few seconds. (This will help stop the peel from sticking to the bottom of the dough.) Then, carefully slide it under the pide and turn it 180 degrees. When the top of the pide that is now at the back of the oven starts to brown/blister, turn the pide again, but this time, 90 degrees. Finally, do one last 180-degree turn so that all the pide has an even bake. The total cooking time should be approximately 1½ to 2 minutes.

Remove the pide from the oven and slide onto a cooling rack for 1 to 2 minutes before transferring to a display board. Repeat for the second pide. Depending on how many guests you have, cut horizontally across the central seam into an appropriate number of pieces and serve hot.

PIZZA CANNOLO
(AKA THE DOG BONE PIZZA)

YIELD: 1 pizza (serves 1-2)

84 g (¾ cup) fresh mozzarella, divided
1 (275-g) ball Neapolitan Dough (page 19)
1 tbsp (14 g) ricotta
1–2 tbsp (15–30 ml) Keep-It-Simple Tomato Sauce (page 35)

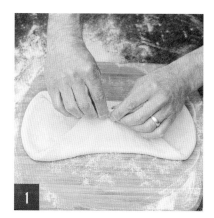

This pizza is inspired by sweet Italian pastries known as cannoli Siciliani. These are a staple of Italian cuisine made using fried pastry dough with sweet, creamy fillings. This savory version uses Neapolitan pizza dough in place of the fried pastry and makes a fun change from a standard round pizza. One of the things I like most about this pizza is that it is basically two mini pizzas and a calzone all in one! When I was going through the process of deciding which recipes to include in this book, I knew straight away this would be one of them, but the biggest decision I had to make was whether to go with "The Bow Tie Pizza" or "The Dog Bone Pizza." I went with the latter, because when I made this for the first time, I remember my dog, Ronnie, paying very close attention to it!

To keep the pizza cannolo from getting soggy, remove as much moisture from the fresh mozzarella as possible by breaking it into small pieces and laying them down onto a few layers of paper towels at least 1 hour before cooking. To help draw out even more moisture, lay another paper towel on top as well.

Fire up your Ooni pizza oven, and aim for a stone temperature of 715 to 750°F (380 to 400°C). Depending on the outside temperature, this should take approximately 15 to 20 minutes. In the colder months, an extra 10 to 15 minutes might be needed. You can check the stone temperature with an infrared thermometer.

When the stone has reached approximately 660°F (350°C), stretch out the dough ball using the instructions on page 21.

Add the ricotta and 30 grams (⅓ cup) of the mozzarella in the middle of the dough. Lift both sides of the dough, moving them to the center until they meet, and pinch the sides together to create a seal. You want this sealed section to be approximately 3 to 4 inches (8 to 10 cm) long (refer to photo 1).

(continued)

PIZZA CANNOLO (AKA THE DOG BONE PIZZA) (CONTINUED)

Fresh basil leaves, soaked in salt water*

1 tsp finely grated Grana Padano

15 g sliced pepperoni

Drizzle of extra virgin olive oil

Fine semolina flour

* Soaking the basil leaves in salt water protects them from burning, since they are added before baking.

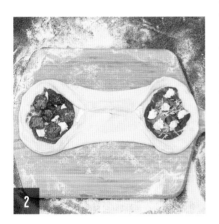

Add the tomato sauce to the center of the base on each side and spread in a circular motion, moving out toward the crust using the back of your spoon. Add the basil leaves, Grana Padano and remaining mozzarella to each side before adding the pepperoni to just one side. Finish with a drizzle of oil on both sides (refer to photo 2).

Give your chosen pizza peel a light dusting of semolina flour before transferring the dough onto it. You can do this by lying the peel flat alongside the dough, and then, using both hands, gently lift the edge of the dough and slide it onto the peel. This stage can be daunting, but be confident and do it in one smooth, quick movement. After sliding the dough onto the peel, give it a final reshape. If you don't feel confident enough to use this technique, you can place the stretched-out dough straight onto the floured peel after stretching it over your knuckles and shape/top it while on the peel.

When the stone temperature has reached 715 to 750°F (380 to 400°C), give the peel a little shuffle/shake to ensure the dough isn't sticking, and then launch confidently into the middle of your Ooni pizza oven.

After approximately 20 seconds, you will begin to see the crust at the back of the oven start to brown/blister. Warm the metal peel/turning peel in the back of the oven by holding it in the flames for a few seconds. (This will help stop the peel from sticking to the bottom of the pizza.) Then, carefully slide it under the pizza and turn it 180 degrees. When the crust that is now at the back of the oven starts to brown/blister, turn the pizza again, but this time, 90 degrees. Finally, do one last 180-degree turn so that all the pizza has an even bake. The total cooking time should be approximately 90 seconds.

Remove the pizza from the oven and slide it onto a cooling rack for 1 to 2 minutes before transferring to a display board. Cut and serve hot.

A SPICY STAR IS BORN

YIELD: 1 pizza (serves 1-2)

112 g (1 cup) fresh mozzarella

1 (275-g) ball Neapolitan Dough (page 19)

Fine semolina flour

30 g 'nduja, broken into small pieces

2–3 tbsp (30–45 ml) Keep-It-Simple Tomato Sauce (page 35)

1 tsp finely grated Grana Padano

Drizzle of extra virgin olive oil

Fresh basil leaves

When it comes to making pizzas that are a bit out of the ordinary, the star-shaped pizza is my all-time favorite, and the one I make most often. Perfect as a sharing centerpiece, be sure to serve this up the next time you have friends and family over. No matter what other pizzas you place down on the table, the first thing your guests will do is tear off one of the spicy, gooey stuffed star points. This is an extremely versatile pizza where you can really experiment with toppings and fillings. You could even mix things up and use a different filling in each of the eight star points. The possibilities are endless! It can be difficult to achieve a nice symmetrical shape, but the biggest piece of advice I can give is to make sure that all 8 cuts you make into the stretched-out dough are the same length and no longer than the specified 1½ inches (4 cm). This will help the dough hold its shape when it comes to launching into your Ooni pizza oven.

To keep the pizza from getting soggy, remove as much moisture from the fresh mozzarella as possible by breaking it into small pieces and laying them down onto a few layers of paper towels at least 1 hour before cooking. To help draw out even more moisture, lay another paper towel on top as well.

When your dough ball has rested for 4 to 6 hours at room temperature (or 3 hours after removing it from the fridge), fire up your Ooni pizza oven, aiming for a stone temperature of 750 to 800°F (400 to 430°C). Depending on the outside temperature, this should take approximately 15 to 20 minutes. In the colder months, an extra 10 to 15 minutes might be needed. You can check the stone temperature with an infrared thermometer.

When the stone temperature has reached approximately 715°F (380°C), tip out your dough ball from the container (or remove it from the dough tray) onto a bed of fine semolina flour. (If you don't have fine semolina, you can use normal 00 flour that you used to make your dough.) Cover the dough with some extra semolina so it is coated and not sticky to touch. If the dough has lost its circular shape, reshape it at this point. From the center, using your fingers, carefully push the dough down and out, going all the way to the edge. Do not leave any crust (refer to photo 1 in Tonda Romana dough recipe on page 33).

(continued)

A SPICY STAR IS BORN (CONTINUED)

Keep rotating the dough as you do this to maintain its circular shape as this will impact the final shape of your pizza once it is cooked. Flip the dough over and continue to stretch it out using this technique. From this point make sure you don't flip the dough over again as this is the side we want as the top of the pizza. (This was the side that was at the top when in the container.) Once the dough has been stretched as far as possible using this technique, pick the dough up and carefully toss it from one hand to the other a few times to remove some of the excess flour. Hang the dough up right over both sets of your knuckles and rotate the dough through your hands, allowing gravity to stretch it out (refer to photo 6 in Neapolitan dough recipe on page 21).

Make sure it is the outer edge that hangs off your knuckles. It's important not to stretch from the center as this will make the base too thin, causing it to tear. Once the dough is evenly stretched to about 11 inches (28 cm) with a nice, thin base, place it down straight onto a floured peel. Using your fingertips, gently press down around the edge to make sure it is nice and flat. As you will be forming the shape and topping directly on a peel, I recommend using a little bit more flour on the peel to make sure it doesn't stick. Using a pizza cutter, make 8 equally spaced 1½-inch (4-cm) cuts into the dough (refer to photo 1).

Add small pieces of mozzarella and 'nduja to each of the 8 sections. It's important not to use too much as it could make sealing these sections difficult. Carefully lift the two corners of one section and pinch together while moving it toward the center of the pizza. Next, pinch together the remaining area of the star point. Repeat this for the remaining sections (refer to photo 2).

Between each of the 8 star points, carefully pinch the dough with your fingers to form a shallow wall. This will help contain the tomato sauce and stop it leaking onto the stone when cooking (refer to photo 3).

Add the tomato sauce to the center of the base and spread in a circular motion, using the back of your spoon. Next, evenly add the Grana Padano, the remaining fresh mozzarella and 'nduja before a drizzle of oil (refer to photo 4).

When the stone temperature has reached of 750 to 800°F (400 to 430°C), give the peel a little shuffle/shake to ensure the dough isn't sticking, and then launch confidently into the middle of your Ooni pizza oven. Do not take your eyes off the pizza, as a few seconds can make a big difference to the overall bake!

After approximately 20 to 30 seconds, you will begin to see the star points at the back of the oven start to brown/blister. Warm the metal peel/turning peel in the back of the oven by holding it in the flames for a few seconds. (This will help stop the peel from sticking to the bottom of the pizza.) Then, carefully slide it under the pizza and turn it 180 degrees. When the star points that are now at the back of the oven start to brown/blister, turn the pizza again, but this time, 90 degrees. Finally, do one last 180-degree turn so that all of the star pizza has an even bake. The total cooking time should be approximately 90 seconds.

Remove the pizza from the oven and slide it onto a cooling rack for 1 to 2 minutes before transferring to a display board. Neatly add the basil leaves to the center. Cut into 8 slices and serve hot.

GARLIC DOUGH STRIPS

YIELD: 1-2 servings

For the Strips
1 (275-g) ball Neapolitan Dough (page 19)

Fine semolina flour

Everyone has heard of, and most probably tried, dough balls at some point in their life, but I present to you: Garlic dough strips. Not only are these nicer (in my opinion), but they're actually simpler to make than dough balls. The super-high temperature inside your Ooni pizza oven will have these rising instantly, creating beautiful soft strips of dough. The first time I made these, I knew they were going to be special, so before I served them to the rest of my family that day, I sneaked my daughter into the kitchen so that she could be the first person to try them. I will never forget the look of pure joy on her face after that first bite. It's little moments like these that make it all worthwhile and show just how much happiness pizza can bring to people's lives. I guarantee that if you serve these to your friends and family, they will be talking about them for a long time to come.

When your dough ball has rested for 4 to 6 hours at room temperature (or 3 hours after removing it from the fridge), fire up your Ooni pizza oven, aiming for a stone temperature of 800 to 840°F (430 to 450°C). Depending on the outside temperature, this should take approximately 20 minutes. In the colder months, an extra 10 to 15 minutes might be needed. You can check the stone temperature with an infrared thermometer.

When the stone temperature has reached approximately 750°F (400°C), tip out your dough ball from the container (or remove it from the dough tray) onto a bed of fine semolina flour. (If you don't have fine semolina, you can use normal 00 flour that you used to make your dough.) Cover the ball with some extra semolina so the whole dough is coated and not sticky to the touch. If the dough has lost its circular shape, reshape it at this point.

From one side, using the palm of your hand, carefully press down on the dough, moving along until you reach the opposite side, going all the way to the edge. (Do not leave any crust.) Repeat this technique (also going from the top to bottom) until you have an oval that is approximately 7 x 10 inches (18 x 24 cm).

(continued)

GARLIC DOUGH STRIPS (CONTINUED)

For the Garlic and Herb Butter

28 g (2 tbsp) softened salted butter

2 cloves garlic, crushed or finely chopped

1 tsp dried parsley or rosemary

Give your chosen pizza peel (I recommend using a wooden or solid metal peel as we will be cutting the dough into strips directly on the peel) a light dusting of semolina flour before transferring the flattened dough onto it. You can do this by laying the peel flat alongside the dough, and then, using both hands, gently lift the edge of the dough and slide it onto the peel. This stage can be daunting, but be confident and do it in one smooth, quick movement. After sliding the dough onto the peel, give it a final reshape. With a pizza cutter, cut the dough into equal-sized strips that are approximately 1½-inch (4-cm) wide (refer to photo 1).

When the stone temperature has reached 800 to 840°F (430 to 450°C), give the peel a little shuffle/shake to ensure the dough isn't sticking, and then launch confidently into the middle of your Ooni pizza oven. Do not take your eyes off the strips, as a few seconds can make a big difference to the overall bake!

After approximately 20 to 30 seconds, you will begin to see the ends of the dough strips at the back of the oven start to brown/blister. Warm the metal peel in the back of the oven by holding it in the flames for a few seconds. (This will help stop the peel from sticking to the bottom of the pizza.) Then, carefully slide it under the dough strips and remove them from the oven. Place your peel down onto a flat surface, and using your hands, carefully turn the dough strips 180 degrees before launching them back into the oven. When the ends of the dough strips that are now at the back of the oven start to brown/blister, remove them from the oven and slide onto a cooling rack for 1 to 2 minutes. The total cooking time should be 60 to 90 seconds.

While the dough strips are on the cooling rack, make the garlic and herb butter. Melt the butter in the microwave, and in a small bowl, mix together the butter, garlic and parsley. Transfer the dough strips to a plate while they are still hot and pour the melted garlic and herb butter all over. Serve immediately.

PIZZA DAWGS

YIELD: 2 dawgs (serves 1-2)

56 g (½ cup) fresh mozzarella
2 hot dogs or standard sausages
1 (275-g) ball Neapolitan Dough (page 19)
Fine semolina flour
Drizzle of ketchup
Drizzle of yellow mustard
Sprinkle of store-bought crispy onions

Do you ever struggle to decide whether to make hot dogs or pizza? Well, look no further, as this recipe combines the two, giving you the best of both worlds. I'm extremely confident that once you have made these you won't be going back to normal hot dogs. I've gone quite traditional with the hot dog toppings in this recipe, sticking with ketchup, mustard and crispy onions, but you can add anything you like—just let your imagination run wild! You'll notice that the hot dogs are added to the dough halfway through the bake. By doing this, the intense heat from your Ooni pizza oven will make the dough continue to rise and shape itself around the profile of the hot dogs. I'd like to thank a fellow pizza blogger, Luke (aka the Pizza Pilot), as he was the first person I saw make these pizza dogs, and I can safely say I've not looked back since.

To keep the pizza dawgs from getting soggy, remove as much moisture from the fresh mozzarella as possible by breaking it into small pieces and laying them down onto a few layers of paper towels at least 1 hour before cooking. To help draw out even more moisture, lay another paper towel on top as well.

Cook the hot dogs according to the instructions on the packaging. (If you are using standard sausages, cook them in your home oven or in a frying pan until cooked through and just starting to brown on the outside.) Once cooked, allow to cool.

When your Neapolitan dough ball has rested for 4 to 6 hours at room temperature (or 3 hours after removing from the fridge), fire up your Ooni pizza oven, and aim for a stone temperature of 800 to 840°F (430 to 450°C). Depending on the outside temperature, this should take approximately 20 minutes. In the colder months, an extra 10 to 15 minutes might be needed. You can check the stone temperature with an infrared thermometer.

When the stone temperature has reached approximately 750°F (400°C), tip out your dough ball from the container (or remove it from the dough tray) onto a bed of fine semolina flour. (If you don't have fine semolina, you can use normal 00 flour that you used to make your dough.) Cover the ball with some extra semolina so the whole dough is coated and not sticky to the touch. If the dough has lost its circular shape, reshape it at this point.

Gently press down onto the dough ball using the palm of your hand to evenly increase the size of the dough. Cut the dough ball in half with a dough cutter and form each half into oval shapes slightly longer than the hot dogs. Set one half aside as you make your first pizza dawg (refer to photo 1).

(continued)

PIZZA DAWGS (CONTINUED)

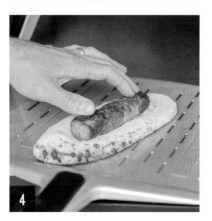

Pick the dough up and carefully toss it from one hand to the other a few times to remove some of the excess flour. Place it down vertically onto a floured peel. Reshape into an extended oval at this point, if required. Starting at ½ inch (1.3 cm) from the bottom, use two fingers to gently press down onto the center of the dough, moving up until you reach ½ inch (1.3 cm) from the top to form a channel (refer to photo 2).

Rotate the dough 180 degrees, and repeat this technique until the channel is roughly the same length as the hot dog. Add the mozzarella into the channel down the middle of the dough (refer to photo 3). This will help keep the center weighed down for you to place the hot dog into halfway through the overall bake. (And let's be honest, adding cheese to anything takes it to the next level!)

When the stone temperature has reached 800 to 840°F (430 to 450°C), give the peel a little shuffle/shake to ensure the dough isn't sticking, and then launch confidently into the middle of your Ooni pizza oven. Do not take your eyes off the dough, as a few seconds can make a big difference to the overall bake!

After approximately 20 seconds, you will begin to see the dough all around the trench start to rise and the dough at the back of the oven start to brown/blister. Warm the metal peel/turning peel in the back of the oven by holding it in the flames for a few seconds. (This will help stop the peel from sticking to the bottom of the dough.) Then, use it to carefully slide under the dough and remove it from the oven.

Push the hot dog firmly into the trench, and turn the dough 180 degrees before launching back into the oven. Try to be quick when doing this, as we don't want the dough to cool down (refer to photo 4).

When the side of the dough that is now at the back of the oven starts to brown/blister, turn the dough again, but this time, 90 degrees. Finally, do one last 180-degree turn so that all the dawg has an even bake. The total cooking time should be approximately 60 to 90 seconds. Remove the dawg from the oven and slide it onto a cooling rack for 1 to 2 minutes before transferring to a display board. Neatly add the ketchup, mustard and crispy onions and serve hot. Repeat all the above steps to make the second pizza dawg.

DELIGHTFUL
DESSERTS

I'll always fondly remember my first-ever dessert pizza experience in a pizzeria close to where I live. Looking over the dessert menu, nestled (almost hidden) right at the bottom, underneath the usuals like chocolate fudge cake and ice cream, was a standard pizza base topped with chocolate spread, marshmallows, sweets and cookies. A life-changing discovery!

One of the best things about dessert pizzas is that you can literally use anything and chances are that it will work. Whether that's fruit, chocolate, sweets, nuts or custard, anything goes! In this chapter, you'll find most of my recipes are based around some form of chocolate (I'm a chocoholic after all), but there's also a fruity custard recipe (Nostalgic Plums and Custard on page 183), which holds special memories of my late grandparents. And while you're at it, why not get creative and make your own recipe with the ingredients found in your favorite dessert dish?

You'll notice that two of the pizzas in this chapter have their toppings added after the pizza base has been baked. This method of baking a base without any toppings is commonly referred to as blind baking. To prevent the base from burning during this process, I use ice cubes. It's important that the ice melts within the first few seconds after launch, so with Ooni pizza ovens being able to reach 930°F (500°C), this makes them perfect for blind baking with ice.

GO NUTS!

YIELD: 1 pizza (serves 1-2)

14 g (2 tbsp) hazelnuts
1 (275-g) ball Neapolitan Dough (page 19)
Fine semolina flour
4-5 ice cubes
42 g (3 tbsp) chocolate hazelnut spread

When chocolate and nuts come together, magic happens! When I think of chocolate and nuts, I picture myself eating my favorite bar of chocolate with hazelnuts. So for this recipe I decided to use these two ingredients to make this wonderful dessert pizza. Before my first attempt at making this pizza, I had never before roasted hazelnuts, but the extra crunchiness, nuttiness and mellow flavor make this extra bit of effort worthwhile. When I first discovered the ice cube method of blind baking a pizza base, this dessert pizza was the first time I put it into practice.

Preheat your home oven to 350°F (180°C).

Lay the hazelnuts evenly on a baking tray and roast for 10 to 12 minutes, or until the skins start to crack. Let them cool for a few minutes before rubbing them with a kitchen towel to release the skins. Roughly chop the hazelnuts and set aside.

Fire up your Ooni pizza oven, and aim for a stone temperature of 800 to 840°F (430 to 450°C). Depending on the outside temperature, this should take approximately 20 minutes. In the colder months, an extra 10 to 15 minutes might be needed. You can check the stone temperature with an infrared thermometer.

When the stone has reached approximately 750°F (400°C), stretch out the dough ball using the instructions on page 21. As we want the base to be slightly thicker (to reduce the likelihood of it tearing), only stretch out the base to 9 inches (23 cm) instead of the instructed 11 inches (28 cm).

Give your chosen pizza peel a light dusting of fine semolina flour before transferring the dough onto it. You can do this by lying the peel flat alongside the dough, and then, using both hands, gently lift the edge of the dough and slide it onto the peel. This stage can be daunting, but be confident and do it in one smooth, quick movement. After sliding the dough onto the peel, give it a final reshape. If you don't feel confident enough to use this technique, you can place the stretched-out dough straight onto the floured peel after stretching it over your knuckles. Evenly space the ice cubes onto the base, making sure one is in the center to prevent the dough from doming and burning in the oven.

(continued)

GO NUTS!
(CONTINUED)

When the stone temperature has reached 800 to 840°F (430 to 450°C), give the pizza peel a little shuffle/shake to ensure the dough isn't sticking, and then launch confidently into the middle of your Ooni pizza oven. Do not take your eyes off the pizza, as a few seconds can make a big difference to the overall bake!

After the launch, if the ice cubes are no longer evenly spaced, use long kitchen tongs and a heatproof oven glove to carefully reposition them.

After approximately 20 seconds, you will begin to see the crust at the back of the oven start to brown/blister. Warm your metal peel/turning peel in the back of the oven. (This will help stop the peel from sticking to the bottom of the pizza.) Then, carefully slide it under the pizza and turn it 180 degrees. When the crust that is now at the back of the oven starts to brown/blister, turn the pizza again, but this time, 90 degrees. Finally, do one last 180-degree turn so that all of the pizza has an even bake. The total cooking time should be 60 to 90 seconds. If at any point the base starts to dome, slide the metal peel/turning peel under the base to release the trapped air.

Remove your pizza from the oven and slide it onto a cooling rack for 1 to 2 minutes before transferring to a display board. Use some paper towels to soak up any excess moisture on the base from the melted ice cubes. Spread the chocolate hazelnut spread onto your base using the back of a tablespoon so it has a nice, even layer all the way up to where the crust starts. Sprinkle the chopped hazelnuts on top to finish. Cut into 4 or 6 slices and serve.

DREAMY CHERRY AND CHOCOLATE

YIELD: 1 pizza (serves 1-2)

For the Cherry Compote

308 g (2 cups) pitted cherries

50 g (¼ cup) sugar

1 tbsp (15 ml) lemon juice

240 g (1 cup) water (optional)

½ tsp cornstarch (corn flour) (optional)

For the Pizza

1 (275-g) ball Neapolitan Dough (page 19)

Fine semolina flour

28 g (2 tbsp) milk chocolate spread, plus extra for serving*

14 g (1 tbsp) white chocolate spread, plus extra for serving*

* Chocolate ganache (page 181) or melted chocolate can be used as an alternative.

A few other food bloggers and I challenged ourselves to use cherries as a main pizza topping. I immediately knew exactly what I was going to make. My mind was instantly taken back to a holiday I had in Tunisia, where every evening, my wife and I would take a walk down to the harbor and indulge in a double-chocolate and cherry crepe from a local food stand. Every time I've eaten cherries with chocolate since that holiday, this memory comes to the forefront of my mind! As this is a dessert pizza where the chocolate base and cherries are added pre-bake, the intense heat inside the Ooni pizza oven will cause them to bubble and fuse together, creating what can only be described as magic! If cherries are out of season or you're a bit short on time, you can use store-bought cherry pie filling, which will work well too.

To make the compote, in a saucepan, add the cherries, sugar and lemon juice, and cook over medium heat, stirring often, for 10 to 12 minutes, or until the cherries start to break down. If needed, add a splash of cold water to the cherries to help break them down. If the compote needs thickening up, just before you take the cherries off the heat, mix ½ teaspoon of cornstarch with a splash of water in a small bowl and stir into the cherries, cooking for 1 minute further. Set aside. The compote can be made ahead of time and stored in the fridge for up to 3 days.

Fire up your Ooni pizza oven, and aim for a stone temperature of 800 to 840°F (430 to 450°C). Depending on the outside temperature, this should take approximately 20 minutes. In the colder months, an extra 10 to 15 minutes might be needed. You can check the stone temperature with an infrared thermometer.

When the stone has reached approximately 750°F (400°C), stretch out the dough ball using the instructions on page 21. As we want the base to be slightly thicker (to reduce the likelihood of it tearing), only stretch out the base to 9 inches (23 cm) instead of the instructed 11 inches (28 cm).

Add the milk chocolate spread to the center of the base and spread in a circular motion, moving out toward the crust using the back of your spoon. Warm the white chocolate spread in the microwave for 5 to 10 seconds before drizzling it over the base. Use the back of a spoon to mix the two chocolate spreads together, making a marble effect. Evenly add the cherry compote on top. To prevent the chocolate spread from burning, it is important to completely cover it with the cherry compote.

(continued)

DREAMY CHERRY AND CHOCOLATE (CONTINUED)

Give your chosen pizza peel a light dusting of fine semolina flour before transferring the dough onto it. You can do this by lying the peel flat alongside the dough, and then, using both hands, gently lift the edge of the dough and slide it onto the peel. This stage can be daunting, but be confident and do it in one, smooth, quick movement. After sliding the dough onto the peel, give it a final reshape. If you don't feel confident enough to use this technique, you can place the stretched-out dough straight onto the floured peel after stretching it over your knuckles.

When the stone temperature has reached 800 to 840°F (430 to 450°C), give the pizza peel a little shuffle/shake to ensure the dough isn't sticking, and then launch confidently into the middle of your Ooni pizza oven. Do not take your eyes off the pizza, as a few seconds can make a big difference to the overall bake!

After approximately 20 seconds, you will begin to see the crust at the back of the oven start to brown/blister. Warm your metal peel/turning peel in the back of the oven. (This will help stop the peel from sticking to the bottom of the pizza.) Then, carefully slide it under the pizza and turn it 180 degrees. When the crust that is now at the back of the oven starts to brown/blister, turn the pizza again, but this time, 90 degrees. Finally, do one last 180-degree turn so that all of the pizza has an even bake. The total cooking time should be 60 to 90 seconds.

Remove your pizza from the oven and slide it onto a cooling rack for 1 to 2 minutes before transferring to a display board. Warm the extra milk and white chocolate spreads in the microwave for 5 to 10 seconds before drizzling over the pizza with a spoon. Cut into 4 or 6 slices and serve hot.

CHOCOLATE ORANGE

YIELD: 1 pizza (serves 1-2)

For the Chocolate Ganache
111 g dark chocolate

60 ml (¼ cup) heavy cream (double cream)

For the Pizza
1 (275-g) ball Neapolitan Dough (page 19)

Fine semolina flour

4-5 ice cubes

Chocolate orange segments

Orange zest, for garnishing

This is a chocolate lover's dream! Chocolate and orange are one of my all-time favorite sweet flavor combinations, so when I started experimenting with dessert pizzas, this was right at the top of the list of pizzas I wanted to make. Most chocolate-based dessert pizzas use a ready-made chocolate spread for the base, but in this recipe, I am going to show you how to take it to the next level by using a silky, smooth chocolate ganache! It is a little bit more involved, but trust me, the extra effort really is worth it. Be sure to have a camera at the ready so you can capture your guests' reactions when you put this pizza on the table, and more importantly, when they take their first bite! This is another dessert pizza where all the toppings are added post-bake, so get those ice cubes ready as you'll be doing another blind bake!

Fire up your Ooni pizza oven, and aim for a stone temperature of 800 to 840°F (430 to 450°C). Depending on the outside temperature, this should take approximately 20 minutes. In the colder months, an extra 10 to 15 minutes might be needed. You can check the stone temperature with an infrared thermometer.

While your pizza oven is heating up, make the ganache. In a bowl, break the dark chocolate up into small pieces. Pour the cream into a saucepan and slowly bring to a simmer, stirring continuously. Once simmering, take it off the heat and carefully add the dark chocolate, stirring continuously until smooth and glossy. Set aside.

When the stone has reached approximately 750°F (400°C), stretch out the dough ball using the instructions on page 21. As we want the base to be slightly thicker (to reduce the likelihood of it tearing), only stretch out the base to 9 inches (23 cm) instead of the instructed 11 inches (28 cm).

Give your chosen pizza peel a light dusting of fine semolina flour before transferring the dough onto it. You can do this by lying the peel flat along-side the dough, and then, using both hands, gently lift the edge of the dough and slide it onto the peel. This stage can be daunting, but be confident and do it in one smooth, quick movement. After sliding the dough onto the peel, give it a final reshape. If you don't feel confident enough to use this technique, you can place the stretched-out dough straight onto the floured peel after stretching it over your knuckles. Evenly space the ice cubes onto the base, making sure one is in the center to prevent the dough from rising and burning once in the oven.

(continued)

CHOCOLATE ORANGE (CONTINUED)

When the stone temperature has reached 800 to 840°F (430 to 450°C), give the pizza peel a little shuffle/shake to ensure the dough isn't sticking, and then launch confidently into the middle of your Ooni pizza oven. Do not take your eyes off the pizza, as a few seconds can make a big difference to the overall bake!

After the launch, if the ice cubes are no longer evenly spaced, use long kitchen tongs and a heatproof oven glove to carefully reposition them.

After approximately 20 seconds you will begin to see the crust at the back of the oven start to brown/blister. Warm your metal peel/turning peel in the back of the oven. (This will help stop the peel from sticking to the bottom of the pizza.) Then, carefully slide it under the pizza and turn it 180 degrees. When the crust that is now at the back of the oven starts to brown/blister, turn the pizza again, but this time, 90 degrees. Finally, do one last 180-degree turn so that all of the pizza has an even bake. The total cooking time should be 60 to 90 seconds. If at any point the base starts to dome, slide the metal peel/turning peel under the base to release the trapped air.

Remove your pizza from the oven and slide it onto a cooling rack for 1 to 2 minutes before transferring to a display board. Use some paper towels to soak up any excess moisture on the base from the melted ice cubes. Add 42 grams (3 tablespoons) of the chocolate ganache onto your base and spread using the back of a tablespoon so there is a nice, even layer all the way up to where the crust starts. Add the chocolate orange segments before finishing with some freshly grated orange zest. Cut into 4 or 6 slices and serve.

NOSTALGIC PLUMS AND CUSTARD

YIELD: 1 pizza (serves 1-2)

For the Stewed Plums
45 g (3 tbsp) brown sugar
30 ml (2 tbsp) water
15 ml (1 tbsp) lemon juice
2–3 plums, pitted and cut into wedges
1 cinnamon stick

For the Pizza
1 (275-g) ball Neapolitan Dough (page 19)
60 ml (¼ cup) custard or vanilla pudding
Fine semolina flour
1 gingersnap (ginger biscuit), crumbled

Stewed plums and custard is a dessert I had a lot growing up. My late grandmother "Nana June" was an incredible cook and was famous for her delicious desserts. Her stewed plums and custard was undoubtably one of her best, so I have created this recipe to honor her. On Sundays, we would always go to Nana and Grandad's for a roast dinner, and to add to the excitement, they kept what the dessert was a secret until we arrived. Walking into their kitchen and smelling those sweet plums gently stewing away always brought a huge smile to my face. This was also a dessert my grandparents worked on together as a team (teamwork makes the dream work), with Nana on the plums and Grandad in charge of the all-important custard. The combination of the sweet plums, rich and creamy custard and a little bit of crunch from the crumbled ginger biscuits will have your taste buds tingling!

Note: If you are unfamiliar with custard, it is a thick, creamy, sweet dessert made using egg yolks, milk, vanilla, sugar and cornstarch (corn flour). It is also referred to as crème Anglaise or pudding (in America) and can be found in most supermarkets.

Fire up your Ooni pizza oven, and aim for a stone temperature of 800 to 840°F (430 to 450°C). Depending on the outside temperature, this should take approximately 20 minutes. In the colder months, an extra 10 to 15 minutes might be needed. You can check the stone temperature with an infrared thermometer.

While your pizza oven is heating up, make the stewed plums. Place the brown sugar, water and lemon juice in a saucepan and heat over medium heat, stirring frequently, for 1 to 2 minutes, or until the sugar has dissolved. Add the plum wedges and cinnamon stick, and cook for 8 to 10 minutes, or until tender. Set aside to cool. Don't discard the syrup!

When the stone has reached approximately 750°F (400°C), stretch out the dough ball using the instructions on page 21. As we want the base to be slightly thicker (to reduce the likelihood of it tearing), only stretch out the base to 9 inches (23 cm) instead of the instructed 11 inches (28 cm).

Add the custard to the center of the base and spread in a circular motion, moving out toward the crust using the back of your spoon. Evenly add the plums on top of the custard. Be sure to save the syrup from the stewed plums to drizzle on post-bake.

(continued)

NOSTALGIC PLUMS AND CUSTARD (CONTINUED)

Give your chosen pizza peel a light dusting of fine semolina flour before transferring the dough onto it. You can do this by lying the peel flat alongside the dough, and then, using both hands, gently lift the edge of the dough and slide it onto the peel. This stage can be daunting, but be confident and do it in one smooth, quick movement. After sliding the dough onto the peel, give it a final reshape. If you don't feel confident enough to use this technique, you can place the stretched-out dough straight onto the floured peel after stretching it over your knuckles.

When the stone temperature has reached 800 to 840°F (430 to 450°C), give the pizza peel a little shuffle/shake to ensure the dough isn't sticking, and then launch confidently into the middle of your Ooni pizza oven. Do not take your eyes off the pizza, as a few seconds can make a big difference to the overall bake!

After approximately 20 seconds, you will begin to see the crust at the back of the oven start to brown/blister. Warm your metal peel/turning peel in the back of the oven. (This will help stop the peel from sticking to the bottom of the pizza.) Then, carefully slide it under the pizza and turn it 180 degrees. When the crust that is now at the back of the oven starts to brown/blister, turn the pizza again, but this time, 90 degrees. Finally, do one last 180-degree turn so that all of the pizza has an even bake. The total cooking time should be 60 to 90 seconds.

Remove your pizza from the oven and slide it onto a cooling rack for 1 to 2 minutes before transferring to a display board. Drizzle the plum syrup from the saucepan over the pizza before finishing off with the crumbled gingersnap. Cut into 4 or 6 slices and serve hot.

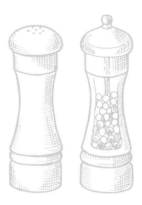

ACKNOWLEDGMENTS

I would like to start by thanking all my family and friends for their incredible support, especially my wife, Nikki, and daughter, Lily. Without them both supporting and encouraging me every step of the way, none of this would have been possible. On top of this, Nikki has also been my photographer for this book. I can't thank you enough for your fantastic vision and for capturing all the amazing photos of my creations. Working together as a family on this book has been so enjoyable and something I will cherish forever.

Special thanks to everyone at Ooni for their continued support and for making my dream of being part of their wonderful team a reality. I thank you all for giving me your blessing to write this book, in which I sincerely hope I have made you all proud. I still pinch myself knowing I'm part of a brand with such genuine and sincere core values.

Next, I would like to thank the incredible online pizza community—an amazing group of like-minded, supportive people who have helped me so much since day one. There are far too many people to mention individually, but all of you know who you are. I am so grateful for every like, comment and interaction you all make with me and my content. I genuinely feel like I have made friends for life.

Big thanks to everyone at Page Street Publishing for believing in me, sharing my vision and making this book happen, particularly Arielle Smolin and Marissa Giambelluca. You have both guided me through the whole process from start to finish making it a such a memorable and enjoyable experience.

I would like to thank Elaine Boddy, who has generously allowed me to tap into her wealth of authoring experience. She is such a kind person who has always been willing to help.

My final thank-you is to my late and dearly missed grandparents, "Nana June" (who this book is dedicated to) and Grandad Ernie. Both were incredibly loving and wonderful people who have been huge role models in my life and have contributed so much to me being the person I am today.

ABOUT THE AUTHOR

Scott Deley is a pizza blogger and all-round pizza enthusiast who created his blog, Scott's Pizza Project, in May 2020 to share his pizza journey and engage with other like-minded enthusiasts. Since then, he has written recipes featured in the Ooni recipe book *Dad's Favourite Recipes*, on the Matthews Cotswold Flour website, as well as being the first overseas guest on the *What's Good Dough?* podcast. His biggest achievement to date came in April 2021, when he proudly became an official brand ambassador for Ooni. This role gives him the perfect platform to do what he loves the most, which is helping others by sharing his experience and knowledge with people all over the world who are on their very own pizza journeys.

Scott lives in Derby, England with his wife, Nikki, and daughter, Lily.

INDEX